HOLISTIC EDUCATION
LEARNING FROM SCHUMACHER COLLEGE

Holistic Education

Learning from Schumacher College

ANNE PHILLIPS

with contributions from Satish Kumar, Fritjof Capra,
David Orr, Vandana Shiva and Wolfgang Sachs

green books

First published in the UK in 2008
by Green Books Ltd, Foxhole, Dartington, Totnes, Devon TQ9 6EB
www.greenbooks.co.uk

in association with

Schumacher College, an initiative of The Dartington Hall Trust
Registered office: The Elmhirst Centre, Dartington, Totnes, Devon, TQ9 6EL
Charity no. 279756 Company no. 1485560

Photos of Leonard and Dorothy Elmhirst on an early visit to Dartington Hall,
Dartington Hall Courtyard before restoration c. 1925, and Rabindranath Tagore with
Ranee Mahalanobis outside the Old Postern in 1926, all © and reproduced with kind
permission of The Dartington Hall Trust Archive (DHTA).
Photos of Maurice Ash, Wendell Berry, Satish Kumar and John Lane
© Kate Mount, reproduced with kind permission of DHTA.
Detail from photograph of Kathleen Jesse Raine by Julia Hedgecoe
© Julia Hedgecoe / National Portrait Gallery, London.
Photo of E. F. Schumacher © Sophie Baker.
Photo of James Lovelock © Sandy Lovelock.
Photo of Manfred Max-Neef © Orla Connolly.
Photo of Satish Kumar and Vandana Shiva together © Alberto Fraile.
Photo of HRH the Prince of Wales during a visit to the College in 2006
© Kate Mount, reproduced with permission of the Prince's Private Secretary.
Photos of Brian Goodwin, Stephan Harding teaching about Deep Ecology, Field trip on
Dartmoor with Stephan Harding, Inge Page, Julia Ponsonby, William Thomas, and of the
College snack area all by Daniel Thistlethwaite © Schumacher College.
Front cover photo by Stephen Prior © Green Books.
Back cover photo of Anne Phillips by Daniel Thistlethwaite © Schumacher College.

ISBN 978 1 900322 36 2

Text printed on 100% recycled paper by TJ International, Padstow, Cornwall, UK

Contents

Acknowledgements

I was commissioned by The Dartington Hall Trust to write this book in order to capture the learning from one of its most recent experiments. Without The Dartington Hall Trust's generous support Schumacher College could never have been opened here in 1991, nor could its continuation have been assured for so long.

My successor as Director of Schumacher College, Karen Blincoe, gave encouragement to my efforts throughout the process of preparing the book. Gratitude and acknowledgement must go to those many individuals, largely unnamed in the text, whose care as staff, voluntary helpers or friends sustain the College. Similarly in the wider community of Dartington and beyond, over the years many people have contributed their creativity and commitment to developing Schumacher College's work.

Staff at The Dartington Hall Trust Archive provided sources for my researches into the history of the Trust's educational activities. Satish Kumar helped design the structure of the book, and in its later stages was tireless in the final refinements. John Lane was ruthless in the early editing and I am sincerely grateful for his incisive and constructive comments on the content and the expression of the work. Vandana Shiva and Wolfgang Sachs kindly made themselves available for interview, and their reflections are encapsulated in the second part of the book.

William Thomas provided insights based on his sixteen years living in the College, as well as many of the photographs, technical support and some text. Heather Gillard and Inge Page (who read the final proofs) were especially helpful as I contacted past participants and teachers. Other staff provided encouragement as the work progressed, and Julia Ponsonby offered pictures from her own records. Numerous former students gave me details about their current work; to all of them I give my thanks and assure them that their efforts were not wasted.

We have tried to ensure that permissions were received for all the photos used in the book; please let the publishers know of any errors and omissions. My friend Sue Greenhalgh proofread the text. John Elford, the publisher, guided me gently through the processes leading to completion of the book.

Nevertheless, in spite of all this help, I must take responsibility for both the opinions in the book and the way they are expressed.

Foreword

by David Green

The creation of Schumacher College in 1991 marked a point of renewal for The Dartington Hall Trust with a fresh focus on values and a 'big idea'. In the wider world, on the one hand were the emerging interrelated systemic disciplines of Complexity theory, Chaos theory and Gaia theory, and on the other an emerging spiritual understanding of ecology represented in the philosophies of Gandhi, Tagore and Deep Ecology. The coupling of ecology and the sacred within Schumacher College was and remains a purposeful and powerful response to the damage being caused in the world by the prevalence of materialism. For the past seventeen years the college has provided space, practice and discourse for those seeking personal transformation in their relationship with and understanding of nature.

The learning at Schumacher College is focused on process rather than on the end product. The emphasis on process is a theme carried over from Dartington Hall School, which closed in 1987 and from whose ashes the College arose. The Gandhian philosophy of learning at different levels and the Tagorean principles of 'practice research' are powerful tools in the personal transformation of those who attend the College. Staff and participants – as a single community – interact and share in the gardening, cooking, cleaning and reflection that form the rhythms of the day. The power and gravitas of the model has attracted pioneering scholars and thinkers from around the world to teach and participate in the learning.

Anne Phillips was there at the founding of the College, and was Director from 1993 through to 2006. There are few people better placed to reflect on the College's origins, its evolution, its processes, its successes and failures. Positioning this within broader currents at Dartington and in wider society emphasises the innovative nature of what Schumacher College sets out to do, how it has adapted, and provides space to speculate on its future. Under her direction, the College expanded beyond the short courses with their range of scientific, practical and esoteric content, to the establishment of a Masters Programme in Holistic Science, the first of its kind.

Today Schumacher College stands on a new threshold. The College has established an international reputation, has maintained and built its integrity, and is a point of reference for many. Now it is time to build upon this work offering transformative learning for sustainable living and working.

David Green
Chairman of the Dartington Hall Trustees

Introduction

A unique learning experience

by Fritjof Capra

Schumacher College grew out of a global environmental movement that had its roots in the counterculture of the 1960s, had flourished in the 1970s and 1980s, and became a central part of the global civil society that emerged during the 1990s. Thus, from the beginning its faculty has been part of an international network of scholars and activists, a network of friends and colleagues that has existed for several decades. It is a centre of learning that largely operates outside leading academic institutions, business organisations and government agencies.

Until 1991 there was no centre of learning where ecology could be studied in a rigorous, in-depth way and from many different perspectives. And as far as the faculty was concerned, none of these scholars and activists had a place where they could explore their ideas and have them critically examined in the relaxed environment of a community that shared their basic values. During the subsequent years, an impressive global coalition of NGOs, now known as the global justice movement or the global civil society, formed around the core values of human dignity and ecological sustainability.

From the very beginning the founders had the vision that the College should not represent a Eurocentric view, but should give voice to a broad range of opinions – that it should be international. When Americans and Europeans discuss science, technology and philosophy here, they are also joined by voices from Africa, India, Japan and other parts of the world.

Another key characteristic of Schumacher College is the strong sense of community it engenders. Participants come here for several weeks to live together, to learn together and also to work together to sustain the learning community. They are divided into working groups that cook, clean, garden – doing all the work that is needed to maintain the College. In these groups, conversations go on virtually round the clock. While they are cutting vegetables in the kitchen, they talk; while they are mopping the floor, or rearranging chairs for a special event, they talk. Everybody here is immersed in a continual experience of community and exciting intellectual dialogue and discussion based on shared values that are deeply ecological and ultimately spiritual.

All this stimulates tremendous creativity. At Schumacher College many things are created collectively, from meals in the kitchen to ideas in the classroom. Creativity flourishes because there is total trust in the community. By nurturing community a climate of trust is created that becomes a fertile ground for creativity.

Schumacher College has created a unique learning environment where discussions take place in an atmosphere that is intellectually very intense and challenging, but is emotionally very safe. When I teach at the College, I feel almost like being among family, and this strong feeling of community emerges after being together for not more than a week or so. To most scholars such a situation is extremely attractive. For we who teach here this is a unique place to examine our work in depth and to try out new ideas in a safe environment.

Fritjof Capra
Summer 2007

Preface

Study at Schumacher College

by Satish Kumar

The same stream of life that runs through my veins night and day
runs through the world and dances in rhythmic measures.
It is the same life that shoots in joy through the dust of the earth
in numberless blades of grass and breaks in tumultuous
waves of leaves and flowers.
It is the same life that is rocked in the ocean-cradle of birth and of
death, in ebb and in flow.

– Rabindranath Tagore, *Gitanjali*

The Schumacher College curriculum is based on the pedagogy of wholeness. Here all learning and teaching is designed on the principles of relatedness and interconnectedness of all subjects and disciplines: science is connected to spirituality, economy to ecology, philosophy to practice and so on.

From the beginning it was realised that a subject-object divide leads to the fragmentation, separation and disconnection which is at the root of the environmental and spiritual crisis facing the world today.

As Einstein said, we cannot solve the problem with the same mindset which created the problem in the first place. So, if the root cause of the multiple crises facing humanity today, such as global warming, social injustice, and economic inequity is the worldview of division and disconnection, then compartmentalised and specialised education is only going to further exacerbate the situation of the already unsustainable economic and political systems around the world.

Almost all higher education is divided into departments and specialisations as this was the design which suited the industrial, mechanistic and materialistic paradigm of progress and development which has perpetuated the undermining of social cohesion and led to the destruction of the biosphere. The need for holistic learning is apparent.

In 1990, when I was invited to be the first Director of the College with the responsibility of designing a holistic study programme, I went to see James Lovelock, the author of Gaia Theory, and asked him to be the first Scholar-in-Residence at the college and lead a five-week long course on Holistic Science. James was reluctant:

"I am an inventor, not a teacher!" said James.

"I know, but where are the teachers who can teach science in a trans-disciplinary manner? Please suggest one," I asked. James could not think of anyone. After a long conversation I was able to persuade him to take part. I said to him, "It is not a question of studying science in an academic way. I would like you to teach science as an inventor and practitioner rather than as a dry theoretician or an academic."

Everyone at the college was pleased that we would be launching the College and our study programme with James Lovelock as the first Scholar-in-Residence, teaching Gaia Theory. In the College's first opening lecture James said, "There are many scientists, economists, sociologists and politicians who stand up for the rights of humans but I stand up for the rights of the species other than humans: the rights of worms, wasps, and birds, the rights of fungi, microbes and bacteria. The Earth is a living system and we need to revere her and not just use her to meet human needs."

In the remaining five weeks he analysed and explained how the Earth acts as a living organism and how she is a self-organising, self-managing and self-correcting whole system and not a collection of fragmented objects. This was a radical science. Darwinian evolution was being updated on this course!

Other teachers we approached were of a similar quality. I met my friend Fritjof Capra, who had been a regular contributor to *Resurgence*, at Paddington Station for a cup of tea to ask him whether he would join the visiting faculty of the college. I was keen to have Fritjof teaching at the College. He brought the science of East and West together and synthesised it in his first book, *The Tao of Physics*, which became an international bestseller. He has made a great impact on scientists and non-scientists alike who were looking for a systemic approach to life, society and nature. He agreed to become a regular member of the faculty of the college and ever since he has been generating ideas, arguments and theories which have led to a number of new courses and new books, including his latest work on the science of Leonardo da Vinci.

Similarly Rupert Sheldrake, a Cambridge biologist, had made waves by writing his ground-breaking book, *A New Science of Life*. The scientific reviewer of *Nature* magazine proclaimed that if there was a case for burning a book, Sheldrake's *A New Science of Life* was a good candidate.

Sheldrake integrated science and spirituality. As Einstein said, science without spirituality is blind and spirituality without science is lame. Sheldrake embodied Einstein's ideas and showed that there is no incompatibility between empirical scientific research and human intuition and spirit. His research showed that all life, human and other than human, is endowed with memory and morphic resonance; life unfolds from within.

In fact science and spirituality need each other. Science without spiritual values can be exploited by military and commercial interests and can lead to the production of nuclear weapons and genetically engineered seeds for example. Spirituality without science on the other hand can end up as dogmatism and fundamentalism and can lead to crusades and holy wars! Thus, integrating science and spirituality has been one of the underlying principles of the Schumacher College programme.

We knew that science not only dominates the educational field but it also informs much of social, political and industrial decision-making: Schumacher College could not ignore the study of science. But mechanistic, reductionist, and materialistic science is not the only kind of science; there is a science of connectivity and wholeness; the qualitative science balancing the quantitative science. There are a large number of exponents of holistic science worldwide who are working in the field of Goethean, and Gaian science who accepted our invitation to teach at Schumacher College.

Our own resident ecologist, Stephan Harding, taught with James Lovelock on the first course and has had a close personal and scientific association with him ever since. Stephan has developed his own brand of Gaian science which he expounded in his book, *Animate Earth*. He has been challenging orthodox science and inspiring students to understand and appreciate natural phenomena as an unbroken living whole. His approach combines rigorous quantitative science with a deep appreciation of the intrinsic value of the natural world. His teaching challenges students to use their factual knowledge about the Earth to develop a deeply felt sense of belonging to the Gaian community of life, air, rocks and water. Time spent outdoors is a very important aspect of his teaching.

Science at Schumacher College is taught not only in the classroom, but also in the field. To develop eco-intelligence we have to learn not only about nature but also from nature. As Thomas Aquinas said, "Revelation comes in two volumes – the Bible and Nature." Going out and being in the wild is an essential part of the design of our study programme. Every week course participants go to Dartmoor and other natural sites to experience the wonder, the mystery, the majesty and the beauty of the wild. These field trips are usually led by Stephan Harding and offer an opportunity to connect with the natural world through studies of Gaia and Deep Ecology. During these trips participants can develop a sense of deep experience, deep identity, deep relationship with and deep reverence for all life, human and other-than-human, upon the earth which can lead to a deep commitment to care for Gaia.

At every opportunity outdoor or indoor, we view nature not merely as an object of study, but as a mentor. Wendell Berry, a noted American visionary poet and writer, led a five-week course on Nature as Teacher. Also, Janine Benyus, a radical scientist and author of the ground-breaking book *Biomimicry*, has run a number of courses in a similar spirit. David Ehrenfeld, professor of biology at Rutgers University and author of the seminal book, *The Arrogance of Humanism*, also emphasised the need for 'ecological humility' on his course. Humberto Maturana extended this 'humility' even further on his course; he introduced the concept of the 'biology of love'. It was wonderful to hear a scientist putting those two words together!

The holistic study of science at Schumacher College became so prominent and popular that in 1998 we were able to launch a Masters programme in Holistic Science accredited by the University of Plymouth with Brian Goodwin and Stephan Harding as the main tutors.

Brian Goodwin, a professor of biology with the Open University, had just retired. When I heard about his retirement I went to see him in Milton Keynes.

"You don't just want to retire; you have so much to contribute! How about accepting the position of Resident Faculty at Schumacher College to launch a new Masters Programme in Holistic Science?" I asked. Brian was attracted immediately to the idea of working with a small community of dedicated students whose aim in life was not just to pass exams, acquire a degree and earn a lucrative salary, but who were passionate about studying science as a way of serving the Earth.

Thus in 1998 and parallel to our short courses, we launched a year-long, full-time, MSc programme which has proved popular and innovative. With Brian and Stephan at the helm the Masters Programme in Holistic

Science has gone from strength to strength. Even though the numbers of students are small, the high quality of teaching and research is making a significant contribution to the development of new ways of knowing and understanding the world.

The holistic approach to science at the college does not do away with the traditional scientific methods of empiricism or reductionism. These methods have their place but students and teachers at the college go further and wider to include a science of qualities, as much as the quantitative approaches of complexity, chaos and Gaia theories. Students seek to understand how their research is relevant to social, environmental, and political issues and how science needs to be studied and practised within the context of ethics, aesthetics and the arts. So nothing is discarded or excluded and everything is considered and included. The study of science at Schumacher College is truly a transdisciplinary procedure. It is a search for meaning in an uncertain world.

In addition to establishing a new approach to science, Schumacher College has also initiated the study of economics as a 'sister' of ecology. Most university departments teaching economics never touch ecology. If ecology is ever studied it is in the scientific departments of biology or geology. At Schumacher College ecology and economics are twin sisters; in fact ecology permeates all subjects.

Both the words, ecology and economy, come from the Greek term, OIKOS which means 'home'. LOGOS means 'knowledge' and NOMOS means 'management' so ecology is the knowledge of our planet home and economy is its management. How can one study the management of the home without knowing the home? But no economics department at the universities seems to ask this question.

According to Gregory Bateson seven virulent epistemological errors have come to dominate our way of thinking in general, and our economics in particular. They are:

1. It's us against the environment.
2. It's us against other people.
3. It's the individual (or the individual congregation or individual company, or the individual nation) that matters.
4. We can have unilateral control over the environment and must strive for that control.

5. We live in an infinitely expanding 'frontier'.
6. Economic determinism is common sense.
7. Technology will do it for us.

The study of economics at Schumacher College attempts to address these errors.

Of course E.F. Schumacher, after whom the college is named, was an economist and wrote about the importance of ecological and spiritual values in economic management. In his famous essay, 'Buddhist Economics', he was the first person to put these two words together. Indeed ecology is at the core of Buddhist philosophy and spirituality; and Buddhist economics is basically the economics of wellbeing. Hazel Henderson, Jonathon Porritt, Wolfgang Sachs, Juliet Schor, Jerry Mander and Karl-Henrik Robert are among the long list of holistic economists who come to Schumacher College on a regular basis to explore the transdisciplinary nature of economics, embedded in ecological and spiritual values.

The study of economics at Schumacher College is not just a matter of pragmatic management of the economy; rather it is a matter of profound values. "What is the purpose of economics?" we always ask. Is it just growth for growth's sake? Production for the sake of production? Or is it for wellbeing and happiness?

To balance the Western perspective on economics we also have to look at economics from the perspective of the third world and from an indigenous perspective. So we invited teachers such as A.T. Ariyaratne of Sri Lanka, Sulak Sivaraksa of Thailand, Winona La Duke from a native American background, Tewolde Egziabher of Ethiopia, Tariq Banuri of Pakistan, Vandana Shiva of India, Martin Khor of Malaysia and Manfred Max-Neef of Chile.

This way Schumacher College has tried to avoid the Eurocentric worldview of economics which has promoted an anthropocentric perspective of human dominance over natural resources resulting in the power of the market, consumerism, free trade, globalisation and unmitigated exploitation of the people as well as the finite resources of the Earth. The economic theories of Adam Smith, Karl Marx and others have kept the majority of the world population in perpetual poverty and caused climate change, resource depletion and pollution of air, water and land. We need to develop a theory of economics which can lead to ecological sustainability and social wellbeing for the whole of humanity.

We believe that economics is a wholly owned subsidiary of ecology. Therefore, the study of ecology at Schumacher College goes deeper than academic ecology as studied in most universities. It includes philosophy. From the very beginning the ecophilosopher at the University of Oslo and scholar of Gandhi and Spinoza, Arne Naess, was one of the strong influences on the College curriculum. During his residency at the College he raised the flag of deep ecology by establishing the premise of nature and all life having intrinsic value irrespective of their usefulness to humans.

In fact nature is not 'out there', separate from humans. As rivers, forests, animals, mountains and oceans are part of nature, so are humans. The word nature is related to birth. Natal, native, nation and nature all come from the same root; humans are born, therefore humans are an integral part of nature. There is no separation, no dualism, only interconnectedness. The study of ecophilosophy is rooted in the idea of the unity of life manifesting in the millions of forms as biodiversity and cultural diversity.

Closely related to ecophilosophy is the study of ecopsychology. From this perspective the ecological and social crisis is a crisis of desires. "There is enough in the world for everybody's needs, but not enough for anybody's greed", said Mahatma Gandhi. The greed to own nature, to consume more, to possess property and to control others stems from our deep-seated insecurity and fear. Unless we can learn to come to terms with our greed, desire, fear and insecurity no amount of scientific, economic or philosophical theories can bring us a sense of sufficiency, fulfilment and wellbeing. The vision in designing the course programme at Schumacher College has always been to offer the participants a sense of enchantment by incorporating a significant element of psycho-spiritual exploration.

James Hillman, Theodore Roszak, Thomas Moore, Marion Woodman, Stanislav Grof, Terry Tempest Williams, and John Seed were among the champions of ecopsychology and ecospirituality. Essentially these teachers and their courses have provided a context for a sincere quest for coherence in an increasingly confused world.

To bring about such coherence a new kind of leadership is needed. Such leadership is not hierarchical, it is not about dictating from the top. Rather, it is about transforming organisations from within. Margaret Wheatley is one of the most prominent teachers at the College who has initiated courses in Inspired Leadership.

All organisations, be they political, social or business, are living systems and not machines. Nature is creative, humans are creative and so are organisations. There is a 'simpler way' to make a shift from the existing paradigm to a new paradigm and that is to recognise that the future can neither be determined nor predicted; it can only be experienced as it emerges. If we take this approach then leadership can be a source of delight and running organisations and our lives can be less arduous. Then we will find that life moves towards wholeness and coherence.

During every course I myself conduct a Fireside Chat. I explore, with the students, the dimensions of wholeness, spiritual renewal and reverential ecology. However, for me spirituality and institutionalised religion are not the same thing. Religions require a set of beliefs whereas spirituality has no dogmas and no fixed ideologies. Spirituality is about compassionate and relational living. In the ocean of spirituality all the rivers of religions merge.

In my approach at the Fireside Chats and also in designing the programme I have been inspired by two great Indian philosophers. First, Mahatma Gandhi. I learnt from him the paramount power of non-violence and love. This power overrides all other powers.

Conventional environmentalism is driven by the fear o1f doom and disaster whereas Gandhian environmentalism is driven by the love of nature; love of rivers, forests, animals and people. Earth is a living community and all species, humans and other-than-humans, are members of this community. We take care of the Earth and of each other because of our love of the Earth. Non-violence is the guiding principle in maintaining a healthy relationship within the Earth community. Gandhi talked about non-violence to nature, non-violence to oneself and non-violence to others. Based on this teaching I have coined the trinity of soil, soul and society in order to encapsulate the interrelatedness of the ecological, spiritual and social dimensions of education. The French Revolution produced a famous slogan – Liberté, Egalité, Fraternité. It was a great social trinity. But, it left out the natural world altogether. Also, it left out the spiritual and personal dimension. Then, in the 60s and 70s the New Age movement came up with another slogan – a personal trinity: Mind, Body, Spirit. This too left out the natural world as well as the social world. We need a new trinity which integrates the personal, the social and the natural. Soil, Soul and Society could be that new, holistic trinity. During various courses at the College we elaborate on the importance of these three dimensions for a sustainable future, a healthy planet and a just society.

Rabindranath Tagore is my other inspiration. He was also a teacher of Leonard Elmhirst, one of the founders of The Dartington Hall Trust. From Tagore I learned that the power of the imagination underpins the power of non-violence and love.

Tagore was a poet, a musician, a painter, a novelist, a social reformer and educationalist. He believed that we can integrate all these disciplines in our lives. Tagore saw learning and living as a seamless continuum.

Following the examples of Gandhi and Tagore, we designed the day at the college in such a way that intellectual exploration is balanced by practical activities. The kitchen and the garden at the College are as much a classroom as the room where academic discourse takes place. Gandhi's ashram and Tagore's university at Shantiniketan demonstrate the importance of learning by doing. The staff and the students at Schumacher College do the same; we participate in cooking, cleaning and gardening as part of the study.

I myself cook with the students once a week and have been doing so for the past seventeen years, and I consider the kitchen to be a classroom. I am able to communicate, learn and teach while cooking. The bond and friendship established during this time is long-lasting. It is a celebration of food and friendship. The joyful time spent together is unforgettable. And, at the end of the two-hour session we have a delicious meal!

In addition to Gandhi and Tagore there have been many other visionaries whose ideas have informed my planning of the college programme: William Blake, William Morris, Aldo Leopold, Lady Eve Balfour, Ivan Illich, Donella Meadows, David Bohm and Kathleen Raine, to name just a few.

For me it has been an honour and a pleasure to follow in the footsteps of such visionaries and study their work and invite to the College the living visionaries who are actively engaged in transforming the world.

Satish Kumar
March 2008

Chapter 1

The College

"It is wonderful that there is an educational institution in the world that honours and advances E. F. Schumacher's wisdom and legacy. Like his work, Schumacher College is simple, sensible, humane and profound."

– Stephanie Mills, ecological activist and Scholar-in-Residence 1998

In the 1980s The Dartington Hall Trust was known over the world for its educational experimentation, its gardens and its music. Less well known was the crisis it was experiencing as the death of the founders exposed questions about its future direction. Furthermore, one of the key activities of the Trust, The Dartington Hall School, was having problems which the Trustees saw being resolved only by its closure. Whilst this was a huge trauma for the Trust, these two circumstances did create the opportunity for a new educational venture on the Estate.

Schumacher College opened at the beginning of 1991, and by the end of its first decade it had acquired an enviable reputation as a place where the 'new paradigm' was explored, taught and lived. This book is an attempt to tell the complex story of the College's creation and to follow the path of its early development.

The new vision that came to be described as the 'new paradigm' or as an 'ecological and spiritual worldview' was described by Thomas Berry in the late 1980s.[1] He offered a 'larger context of meaning' to our lives, as follows:

'....a new historical vision, the vision of an intimate earth community, a community of all the geological, biological, and human components . . . to guide us on our way to a more creative future. Only in recent times has such a vision become possible. We never knew enough. Nor were we sufficiently intimate with all our cousins in the great family of the earth. Nor could we listen to the various creatures of the earth, each telling its own story. The time has now come, however, when we will listen or we will die. The time has come to lower our voices, to cease imposing our mechanistic patterns on the biological processes of the earth, to resist the impulse to control, to command, to force, to oppress, and to begin quite humbly to follow the guidance of the larger community on which all life depends. Our fulfilment is not in our isolated human grandeur but in our intimacy with the larger earth community, for this is also the larger dimension of our being. Our human destiny is integral with the destiny of the earth.'

– from *The Dream of the Earth*, 1988

Berry's call to action expressed the urgency felt by those inspired by the new ecological and spiritual worldview. It was recognised that society was at a time of deep crisis, which was reflected here in Dartington. It was into this context that Satish Kumar made his original proposal to the Dartington Hall Trustees to set up a Green University to explore the roots of the vision that had brought society to this point, and to look at alternative possibilities for ways towards a more creative future.

This book describes the processes by which Satish's original idea evolved into Schumacher College. It attempts to explain that whilst one person may have an idea, it needs many people to coalesce around it, bringing the different skills and resources that will enable the proposal to be manifest. In the Dartington of the late 1980s, the Trust's earliest educational project had been closed and there was an appetite to establish a new project, building on the interests that had been emerging in recent decades. The general thrust of the idea received sufficient support for approval to be given for initial explorations to begin.

The College was allocated a building owned by The Dartington Hall Trust, the Old Postern, an attractive mediaeval manor house standing in something over an acre of its own grounds. It had been the home of the Rev. Keble Martin, who wrote here his famous book on the flora of the British Isles. The building looks comfortably settled in its south-facing position, nestling into a wooded hillside on the Dartington Hall Estate in south Devon, England. Students almost without exception find the place welcoming, sensing in its various spaces something of its 500 years of history. The Dartington Hall Estate itself covers almost 800 acres of outstandingly beautiful countryside. On the Estate there is a mixed farm, educational buildings, riverside walks and some renowned gardens, all within a stone's throw of the College. A couple of miles away is the ancient market town of Totnes and in opposite directions a little further away are the striking coastline of south Devon and the imposing grandeur of Dartmoor.

The original mediaeval building, which houses all the communal activities of Schumacher College, is adjacent to three small twentieth-century residential buildings which together provide forty-one simple, mainly single bedrooms for the students. Most of the bathroom accommodation is in shared facilities in the residential buildings. There has never been a consensus about whether such facilities accord entirely appropriately with the values and intentions of the College, or whether their simplicity acts as a deterrent to the students who might otherwise come for the courses. The dining room has forty-four dining places, and the kitchen facilities are a good size for about five people to work together to prepare the food for the community. The pans and dishes are just manageable by students, who on the whole are not trained as cooks: for many more diners, the pans would need to be just that bit bigger and so more difficult to handle. The scale of the community living within these parameters does not seem to overwhelm. In fact, most find the scale of the community quite congenial. The College has developed a substantial library of books and some films; there is a craft space, and for those of a musical turn of mind there is a piano standing in the heart of the main building.

By the time the new College opened in January 1991, The Dartington Hall Trust, its sponsor, had already spent £300,000. Much of this had gone on staffing costs, publicity and structural alterations to the Old Postern building to ensure it satisfied statutory requirements for Health and Safety, fire precautions and Health and Hygiene. The College was to be charged a rent by the Trust, at a rate well below a commercial rental – not to pay for these set-up costs, but to contribute to ongoing maintenance.

The staffing costs in its early days were also substantial (£103,000 in the first year) and resulted from the decision of the planning group to pay all staff equally and to peg the rate at that which could have been expected by an academic in a conventional university. As anticipated, in its first year the fee income generated (£93,000) did not even cover the staffing costs. This meant that after also paying for food, heating, publicity costs and funding the visiting scholars' fares and honoraria, the Trust had to subsidise the College by £150,000. It was clear that the College needed to increase earned income if it was to survive and, where feasible, reduce costs. It was largely this simple fact that was to lead to the significant changes after the first two years of College operations (see Chapter 7).

By the end of the first decade, the total annual income to the College had more than doubled to over £200,000, partly as a result of obtaining grant aid, and by letting College space to compatible groups. The annual subsidy required from the Trust dropped to £57,000. Whilst this level seemed sustainable for the Trust, staffing levels were probably too low, and relied upon a level of dedication from staff which was certainly not sustainable.

This financial model is not necessarily replicable anywhere else. The generosity of the Trust has kept the College alive, with some support from other philanthropists. It is difficult to imagine how a similar college could be achieved without an endowment to cover space rental and other costs, or without having to charge fees well beyond the means of most students.

When I stepped down as Director in 2006 I was encouraged to write about the College in such a way that someone who was inspired to establish something like it elsewhere would have some guidance available. I had been a member of the group appointed in the late 1980s to develop the design of what came to be called Schumacher College and since 1993 had been its Director.

This book is my response to that request. I describe the unique circumstances that led to the creation of the College at Dartington. This part is included because my sense has grown over the years that the greatest creativity often occurs in chaotic and seemingly disorganised contexts and where the intellectual soil of the place has been richly tilled. In 1988 that is certainly how Dartington seemed! The period of gestation before the College opened was not easy. Among the original design group there was experience in designing education and training, and an intellectual and emotional understanding of the 'new paradigm', combined with the imagination to visualise a new 'College'. Primarily it was a group of four people who put in the sheer hard work required to muster sufficient support to ensure its realisation.

Much of the book is devoted to the principles underpinning life at Schumacher College and the practices it observed which won it recognition. First there is a description of the particular Dartington context from which this unique college emerged. Generalising from our experiences, there is an exploration of the challenges and paradoxes of trying to work in the 'new paradigm', and a summary of the questions to be posed – and answered – if a place of holistic education is to be created. The last part of the book contains a series of contributions from key environmentalists and educators.

I end most chapters with *Focal points* to draw out the wider implications of the particular story of Schumacher College.

Focal points

- As the Chinese say, a crisis may also be an opportunity. Often such a circumstance provides the best context in which to develop a new idea.
- Chaos is often where creativity occurs.
- A time of creativity is both exhilarating and frustrating, and sadly, potentially disappointing if support is not forthcoming.
- There is a need to keep your nerve, and to be willing to live with uncertainty as the process unfolds.
- As well as developing exciting new ideas, it is vital to grapple with defining the resource needs for a new project as early as possible.

Chapter 2

The Dartington context

"I have always looked on disobedience to the oppressive as the only way to use the miracle of having been born."

– Oriana Fallaci

Historical background

Maps made 1,200 years ago show that the Dartington Estate already existed in much of its present form whilst invaders from mainland Europe were still sailing up the River Dart, burning and pillaging. The Estate was far enough from the sea to escape much of this attention, but upstream their neighbours, the monks at Buckfast Abbey, sometimes disputed the ownership of the salmon in the River Dart. Apart from certain local difficulties, Dartington stayed largely out of the spotlight for the whole of one millennium, with the exception of a period at the end of the fifteenth century when the present Hall was built and its owner, John Holland, was drawn into king-making and war, and paid for his efforts with his life.

If it was far enough away from the centres of power to avoid notice in times of national upheaval such as the Civil War, it could not avoid being affected by the collapse of English agriculture in the nineteenth century, as Europe's colonies began to produce corn to feed the world's growing industrial populations. This marked the beginning of an irreversible decline in the fortunes of the Estate and led to its sale in 1925 to the Elmhirsts.[2]

When Leonard Elmhirst came to view the Estate as the potential home for an experiment in rural regeneration, he at once fell in love with the place. It did not take him long to convince his wealthy new wife, Dorothy, that this was the ideal place for them to realise their new plans together. Soon, almost before any regeneration began in Dartington, they set up an experimental school for, amongst others, Dorothy's children from her first marriage. Dartington's pioneering reputation in the field of education was founded.

Leonard's ideas were largely developed when, as a young man after the first world war he worked in India for the Indian poet, philosopher and social entrepreneur, Rabindranath Tagore.[3] Amongst other projects he set up an experimental school designed to address social and economic issues in rural Bengal. Leonard, a younger son of an impoverished English clergyman and unfit for military service, found himself working in India to 'serve the Empire' during the war. There he had first come across the man who was to inspire much of his work for the rest of his life. Dorothy's background, on the other hand, was different. She was brought up as the only child of an extremely wealthy American. Her mother had died when Dorothy was still a child, and her father had encouraged her to follow her own path to discover her intellectual and cultural interests. She had been inspired by, for example, the social activist and critic John Dewey, and felt a strong sense of responsibility to make some of her personal wealth useful to others in the world. In 1931, Leonard and Dorothy together generously endowed The Dartington Hall Trust, and it is largely on this endowment that projects, one of which was Schumacher College, were founded.

The Elmhirsts' arrival began a new era on the Estate. With their financial resources, their aspirations to set up an experiment in rural regeneration and their inspiration – predominantly from Tagore – their impact was dramatic. They changed the neglected and derelict Estate into a hub of creativity known the world over for its experimentation, its arts and education. Although the Elmhirsts had both been dead some years before Schumacher College was mooted, it is significant that an atmosphere of creativity, experimentation and spirituality still clung to Dartington. The suggestion made in 1988 for a school for ecological and spiritual studies was not immediately thrown out, and eventually found root in this place which had experienced radical experimentation over the previous sixty years.

The Dartington magic

It was the 'magic' of the Estate which attracted Leonard Elmhirst when he first came to view it in 1925, and ever since it has continued to attract a multitude of outstanding individuals – educators, philosophers, artists and scientists as well as thousands of students and visitors who are no less immune to its magic. This quality is easier to feel than to describe.

There is a unique configuration of land, gardens, buildings and architecture. Its history and geography, and the mixture of man-made activities which has evolved over 1,200 years and more, have combined to make a place which inspires the imagination. The Elmhirst experiment began to restore the derelict Estate and created employment for farmers, builders, gardeners, foresters and administrators. They began new agricultural and scientific projects and, unusually for the time, required such new activities to research their work and disseminate the findings. The vitality of such a place was uniquely attractive to the best minds of the time.

The cultural and spiritual heritage that was enriched in the twentieth century at Dartington was based on important nineteenth-century foundations. Then, the clergy living in the Old Postern were centrally involved in contemporary religious and scientific conjecture. James Hillman[4] has said that it is the 'spirit of the(se) ancestors' that has informed much of the work of Schumacher College. Since that period the Trust has attracted numerous artists, craftsmen, philosophers and scientists. Some commentators on Dartington have even argued that it is this cultural heritage that provides the Trust's real capital.

To add to the heady mix of wealth, hospitality and regeneration, there was at the same time a continuing exploration of the tension between democracy or freedom, and autocracy. The governance of institutions was questioned. The first formal headmaster of the school, Bill Curry, wrote extensively about a European Union of States and is credited with being a key inspiration of the current European Union. One of the lessons that the children in the school were expected to learn was about democratic citizenship, and some of the activities on the Estate as a whole were consciously designed to create a common basis for a corporate life.

In Leonard and Dorothy's school, Leonard's own initial educational inspiration seems to have come from the Scout movement. When designing his first school for Tagore in India, he made a visit to check with Lord Baden-Powell whether he could model it on the Scouting movement. There is a record of a small Scout Camp by the River Dart before the Dartington Hall School was opened. For her part, Dorothy had been attracted in the USA by Dewey's teachings. Over the first few years a particular focus for the educational activities at Dartington became clear: a holistic educational approach with a focus on the arts had already become explicit. Their model could be described as progressive, and expressed itself in child-centred learning. 'A school for adventure', it stood for the difference between education *for* life and education *as* life itself.

The combination of all of these aspects of Dartington has always attracted inspiring individuals: artists (some driven out of Germany before the war, such as the Ballet Jooss), the intelligentsia (such as Bertrand Russell) who sent their children to the School, and leading social commentators and philosophers such as Thomas Berry, who were drawn to speak at Dartington's Conferences. In the 60s, 70s and 80s the interests of the then Chairman of the Trustees, Maurice Ash,[5] brought key thinkers about 'the new paradigm' to the Estate. Together such people supported and to some extent prepared the ground for the creation of a centre devoted to the study of the ecological and spiritual worldview.

The educational heritage at Dartington

Dartington Hall School, one of the first activities begun by the Elmhirsts at Dartington was at the forefront of the progressive movement in education, and offered a well-rounded and child-centred experience of both teaching and learning. It was concerned with process, and largely focused on the development of the individual. The learning stressed democratic and participative methodologies.

Leonard and Dorothy's school was truly unprecedented and radical. In order to develop the motley crew of friends and relations they had assembled to staff the school, they brought in a Professor of Education from the United States for five days to guide its design, and within a few weeks the school opened. Leonard brought his experience from setting up a school in Bengal on Tagore's request, and Dorothy contributed her more theoretical understanding from her studies in the States. In contrast to their own schooling, which both had loathed, the new school had an emphasis on the arts and crafts, on projects located across the Estate, on non-academic subjects, on self-expression, on self-government, and the intention to use the Estate as an essential part of the educational process.

This method of learning has been described as learning by doing. Learning by doing or project learning provides a very real kind of knowledge, and it focuses on the doer: but simply *doing* by taking part in the world's business is not necessarily educative. Maurice Ash argued that knowledge about the world is usually learned by abstraction. He said that true education is about wisdom and meaning, and that a stance of doing and interconnectedness is required. The Elmhirsts' school promoted excellence in practical action, ecological rather than instrumental thinking, a balance between masculine and feminine; it studied both science and the arts, and had a focus on meaning. In fact, it had challenged the roots of reductionist knowledge and according to some, provided a model of good educational practice. Maurice Ash, who became Chairman of the Trust after Leonard's death, firmly believed that in the wider society the fragmentation of knowledge and of social life was leading to the systematic destruction of ecology. Yet he believed that progressive education could be criticised because it was in danger of promoting individualism. He argued that Dartington should experiment with what a "holistic and healing" education, as he called it, might be. This perspective had an influence on the establishment of Schumacher College.

A key problem which all the Trust's projects seemed to have had was the expense of supporting private educational experimentation. The first school head agreed about the unsustainability of the costs, and in the 1940s Curry said that "the indispensable conditions for success make us too expensive to serve as a 'model'". Victor Bonham-Carter[6] in the 1950s said that "solvency was not compatible with the educational standards envisaged by the Trustees and Curry". Whilst ruefully acknowledging the costs, people today accept finance as only one reason for any failures of the projects: another was that the mainstream always adopted the best of their practices so there was no longer any call for them to continue.

During the 60s, 70s and 80s there were explicit conversations among the Trustees and others about the future direction of education on the Estate. Additionally people such as Mark Braham[7] and Henryk Skolimowski[8] were brought in to take forward fresh thinking on the Estate. These initiatives were funded privately by Maurice Ash, the Elmhirsts' son-in-law. One of the results was an important conference held in 1964 called 'Who are the Progressives Now?'. Based on this, Maurice Ash edited a book of the same name, and a series of Easter Education Conferences was organised over the following twenty years, with the intention of introducing new ideas into Dartington.

Whilst some consider the Trust's work to be primarily educational, there have never been common views across the Estate of its aims and objectives, but there have been a number of shared beliefs. Identified by

Victor Bonham-Carter, these included a shared commitment to various principles: the renewal of the countryside, the liberty of intellect regardless of class or status, the importance of technical excellence, the absence of prejudice and convention in education, the renewal of the place of the arts in everyday life, and the need for an enlightened and altruistic administration. Not least, it was in the school that such principles were expressed and nurtured.

Schumacher College was to some extent heir to these traditions.

The Education Conferences

Alongside funding the Education Conferences started in the 60s and organised by Mark Braham, Maurice Ash engaged Henryk Skolimowski, an ecophilosopher, as a sort of philosopher-in-residence charged with bringing together elements at Dartington for a centre for spirituality and ecology. Skolimowski designed ecophilosophy and ecotheology conferences between 1978 and 1983. Over the years these lecture series and conferences brought, amongst others, Thomas Berry, Gregory Bateson, R. D. Laing and Arne Naess to Dartington. Satish Kumar also spoke at most of these conferences.

Whilst the Education Conferences of the 60s, 70s and 80s left Dartington's own school and College of the Arts largely untouched, they nevertheless introduced the 'new paradigm' to Dartington. Subjects explored included 'Alternatives for Humanity' in 1977 and 'Images of the Future' in 1978, when Frifjof Capra, James Robertson and Christian Schumacher all spoke. In 1979, at the Conference on 'Thought, Feeling and Intuition', Kathleen Raine spoke to the question 'What is Man?'. In 1981 the Conference title was 'Right Livelihood'; in 1982 'Right Relationships'; in 1983 'Imagination and Reality', and in 1984 'Form and Freedom'. James Hillman contributed a paper on 'Animals in Dreams, Myth and Fairy Tales'. In 1985, the theme was 'The Meaning of Illness'. In later years an educational focus seems to have re-exerted itself, with questions such as 'What future for the Arts?' and 'Imagination, Discipline and Education'.

In November 1986 the first of the Temenos Conferences, 'Art and the Renewal of the Sacred', was held at Dartington, particularly devoted to the Arts of the Imagination. The second and last Temenos Conference at Dartington was held in the following year on 'Art in the Service of the

Leonard and Dorothy Elmhirst on an early visit to Dartington Hall

Dartington Hall Courtyard before restoration, c.1925

Rabindranath Tagore with Ranee Mahalanobis outside the Old Postern in 1926

Maurice Ash

John Lane

E. F. Schumacher

Rachel Carson

Kathleen Raine

Thomas Berry

Satish Kumar

Wendell Berry

James Lovelock

Vandana Shiva

Manfred Max-Neef

Hazel Henderson

Arne Naess

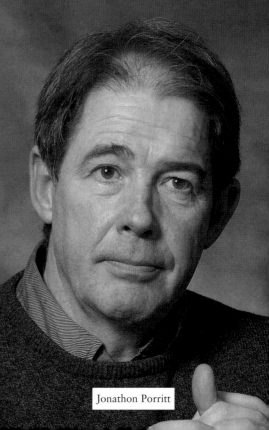

Jonathon Porritt

The Old Postern, home of Schumacher College

The Meditation Room

The College's main central hall

Schumacher College library

The College snack area

Sacred' and was intended, as all others had been, to bring new inspiration to Dartington.

It was during this period that the New Paradigm was being clarified and articulated in the wider world by the key figures that Braham and Skolimowski had invited to Dartington. Here the vision was expressed as an ecological and spiritual worldview and it was understood through the works of the individuals who were eventually invited to teach at Schumacher College.

Focal points

- Schumacher College was not an alien imposition on the Dartington landscape. It has its roots in this place where there had been radical experimentation and exploration in the fields of education, ecology and spirituality going back for more than a century.
- It successfully established itself because it built on, and took forward, these earlier concerns.
- New initiatives or projects stand a better chance of survival if they are rooted in the spirit of their place.

Chapter 3

The ecological and spiritual worldview

It is important to remember that the 60s and 70s were a time of excitement, even euphoria, in the country as a whole. There was a spirit of revolution abroad, and a sense of possibility that illuminated life. A radical critique of the worldview of Modernism was emerging from seminal texts by, amongst others, Edward Abbey, who wrote about his personal experiences in the deserts and mountains of the USA. Wendell Berry, a farmer and poet, wrote about the interdependence of humans and the land in *The Unsettling of America: Culture and Agriculture*. In 1984 Lester Brown and others started to publish an annual report on the basic life systems of the Earth in *The State of the World* series. Fritjof Capra's and Charlene Spretnak's *Green Politics* presented the first evaluation of the political expression of the green movement. Rachel Carson's *Silent Spring* was first published in 1962, and shocked people with its revelation of the poisoning of the land and its consequences. Ivan Illich's *Deschooling Society* in 1983 criticised contemporary institutions and the professions. Thomas Berry's *The Dream of the Earth* in 1988 offered a new vision for our relationship with the Earth. James Lovelock's *Gaia* in 1979 set out clear evidence for considering the Earth a self-regulating system. Bill Mollison's *Permaculture* described a kinder and less disturbing agricultural system. Theodore Roszak's *The Making of a Counter Culture* offered a critique of modern industrial society and pointed towards a more creative and sustainable future.[9]

Perhaps the prospect of the end of the millennium was even then beginning to weave a spell wherein the creation of a new culture and the destruction of the old establishment seemed desirable and even possible. A commitment to this 'new paradigm' was strong amongst a few key people at Dartington by the time Dartington Hall School was threatened with closure during the 1980s. This was the vision that illuminated the thinking for a new college at Dartington. Starting from this small group, a body of support was gradually built for the opening of some kind of academy to explore the foundations of the new vision. By this time it was being described as an ecological and spiritual worldview.

To many the vision was a mystery (and perhaps still remains so), but some seized upon it as a pointer towards a transformation of our relationships with the planet upon which we live and the beings with whom we share it. Yet whilst some may have grasped the meaning of the word 'ecological', there was some discomfort about the use of the word 'spiritual'.

Satish Kumar[10] (the first Director of the College) said to me recently that the purpose of using the word 'spiritual' together with 'ecological' in the descriptions of the College was to indicate that it would pursue non-materialist values: compassion, imagination, creativity, unity of life, ethics and beauty. The design group envisaged a holistic college where the rational, intellectual and scientific aspects should be balanced by intuitive, qualitative and creative dimensions. It was the intention that the College enhance and enrich the soul and spirit, and not be merely intellectual or cerebral. It was not the intention to associate with any particular belief system or religious tradition. By clearly stating that it was a centre for ecological and spiritual studies we were acknowledging the understanding that ecology and spirituality together represent a vision of wholeness.

Most of us never question the fundamental assumptions that underpin the way we, as a culture, live. In the second half of the twentieth century the dominant worldview was based on the powerful, and apparently successful model of Western science. A mechanical analogy was applied to understanding and describing the way the world worked, with the intention of predicting its behaviour and controlling or manipulating the environment. Science focused on breaking things down into their smallest component parts in order to build understanding. Generally, the scientific, philosophical, and economic assumptions which underpinned the apparent success of Western society appeared to be unassailable. On the other hand, it seemed to those persuaded by the ecological perspective that this reductionist approach was not effectively addressing world problems of hunger and disease. Instead it seemed to be leading to the degradation and destruction of the planet's life forms, although at that time the impact of human behaviour on global climate patterns, for example, was not widely accepted. (Incidentally, it is ironic that the picture of Earth taken from space, which became the icon of the green movement, was itself the product of that most emblematic project of Western scientific endeavour – the space mission.)

There were certain ideas or assumptions that coalesced around the ecological and spiritual vision and which were to underpin the work of the College. They were reflected in the first programme that was offered at the College. The work of E. F. Schumacher,[11] best known for his examination of what he called Buddhist Economics, had provided us with a name for the College. (Maurice Ash had suggested that E. F. Schumacher's family might be pleased that the new College would take his name, and they were!) The title of his book *Small is Beautiful* had entered the language as a charm against all that was de-humanising in society, and the body of his work offered a fundamental challenge to mainstream thinking about economics and spirituality, science and psychology.

The College's first courses examined several aspects of new paradigm thinking. First, from the scientific perspective, the essential ecological challenges to the scientific worldview were presented. James Lovelock's Gaia Hypothesis and Rupert Sheldrake's view that the life of nature transcends Western beliefs that nature is inanimate and mechanical, both appeared in the first year's programme. From an economics perspective, we began to explore with Hazel Henderson and Manfred Max-Neef what a more ethical economics would look like: one that satisfied human need and was ecologically and socially sustainable. The role that design had played in creating an environment that disregarded ethics, aesthetics and the ecology of the planet was examined. The recognition that it is individual psychology that creates demand for material satisfaction had led to Roszak's question about what is demanded of us as sane creatures living on a fragile planet, and the College programme began to explore the emerging field of ecopsychology. Examining how the wisdom traditions offer different ways of understanding the world and alternative ways of organising a sustainable society which may be an antidote to the meaninglessness of modern lives, led to trying to understand the philosophy underpinning the old paradigm. Arne Naess, through Deep Ecology, which is a philosophical approach to guiding ethical action (see p.132), considered whether ecologically responsible ways of life are more conducive to the ultimate goals of humanity than ecologically destructive industrial lifestyles. Fritjof Capra looked at a systems view of life, starting from the New Physics and leading on to how to build a sustainable future for the planet. Vandana Shiva came to teach about how science and society have interacted, with science offering technological solutions to social and political problems they have failed to solve. She argued that this elevation of science destroys the sacredness of nature and brings about the loss of traditional ecological knowledge systems.

At the time the College was opened these assumptions were not as clearly articulated as they have since become, but their spirit impacted on the College programme, in the way the spaces in its buildings were designed, and in the practices adopted to run it. Out of the vision of an interconnected and interdependent Earth where people act in an ethically responsible way, there developed a sense that the arts, science and the spiritual were interrelated, and that an education system should aim to illustrate interconnectedness and interdependence if it was to offer a helpful model for living.

One way to describe the approach is to say that the notion of interdisciplinarity grew out of thinking systemically. Taking as the starting point some of the understandings from studies of chaos and complexity, the ecological worldview claimed that Nature is both orderly and predictable *and* unpredictable and creative. The language began to include reference to concepts of the 'emergence of order for free' and the notion that because we live in an interrelated world, life is about relationship. Things simply are, and meaning is in the being. In contrast with the mainstream reductionist view, the concept of wholeness underpins the ecological view, and instead of a search for knowledge there is a striving towards wisdom and understanding. (These were the characteristics of the learning that some had seen in the early school at Dartington.)

The challenge for the College was to translate this new worldview into a curriculum through which to scrutinise the roots of the crisis facing the planet, as we approached the end of the millennium. We needed to search out as teachers, those whose work was challenging conventional wisdom about how to order our lives, and to give them a platform to express and, with others, probe their ideas. Further, and in order to make the learning more effective, in so far as it was possible we were to aim to live out at the College the personal implications of the new worldview we were exposing.

When it opened in 1991 the College was certainly unique in being able to field the distinguished group of individuals who had been recruited as teachers, and in the nature of the learning environment it was able to create.

Focal points

- When the College was first mooted, its agenda reflected a radical critique of the current scientific worldview.
- Underpinning its curriculum was a thoroughgoing and integrated exploration of this critique. The intention was to attempt both to move forward the debate and to live out its implications at a personal level.
- From developing a detailed understanding of the substance of the agenda it becomes possible to identify the detail of the programme and the design of the learning environment.

Chapter 4

Early planning for the College

Just as the winged energy of delight
carried you over many chasms early on,
now raise the daringly imagined arch
holding up the astounding bridges.

Miracle does not lie only in the amazing
Living through and defeat of danger,
Miracles become miracles in the clear
Achievement that is earned.

To work with things is not hubris
When building the association beyond words;
Denser and denser the pattern becomes –
Being carried along is not enough.

Take your well-disciplined strengths
And stretch them between two
Opposing poles. Because inside human beings
Is where God learns.

– Rainer Maria Rilke

With the Trustees' decision to close the School in 1988, Dartington's task was to create something that would fill the vacated building. Primarily this was for pragmatic economic reasons. But some recognised that the real challenge was to re-enspirit the Estate, where the loss of the original educational activity and the death of the founders had left a huge psychological and spiritual gap. The same people realised that setting up a college to explore the new worldview in its own right would satisfy both these needs.

The then Chairman of the Trust, John Pontin,[12] was persuaded by John Lane[13] and Brian Nicholson,[14] the former headmaster of the school, to set up a group of employees and to charge it with finding a way through the crisis.

Trustee John Lane was elected Chair of the group, and recalls that he was always being approached at this time with many ideas for the Trust's future. One of these came from Satish Kumar, the Editor of *Resurgence*, which is a well-established ecological and spiritual magazine. At Maurice Ash's invitation Satish had been contributing during the 60s and 70s to the emerging ideas at Dartington, and he now proposed that the Estate should become home to a new Green University. John Lane knew that the establishment of such a major project was over-ambitious and beyond the resources of the Trust. Nevertheless, it was his task to investigate its feasibility, and he arranged consultations with people in the local community and some from further afield. His personal interests favoured the thrust of the proposal, and it was proposed to the Trustees that it be modified into a form that was realisable within Dartington. From his position as Chair of the Chairman's Group and as a Dartington Hall Trustee, John Lane began to prepare the ground within the Trustee body for this new educational venture.

The Chairman's Group soon set up a committee whose purpose was to consider the possibilities inherent in the suggestion and develop them more realistically into an appropriate form for consideration by the Trustees. In this group, as well as John Lane there were Satish Kumar, Brian Nicholson who had been head of the school when it finally closed, and myself.[15] Kevin Mount, who was trained as a journalist and was employed to promote communication within the Trust, attended all our meetings. He kept records, and helped hone the documents we produced to reflect our proposals. By this time I had worked at Dartington for coming up to two decades, starting originally as a teacher at the school, then moving into staff development in the wider Trust and increasingly into project development. I recently consulted the records from this time. It turns out that I was appointed the Project Manager of this group, and was responsible for co-ordinating the creation and delivery of what was then called 'The School for Complementary Studies'. It was a group with its own powerful momentum and it didn't need much project managing by me!

The Trustees tentatively gave their support to the initiative, but they had reservations about whether there would be a market for the planned courses, and of course about the financial implications. Lord Young of Dartington[16] was a Trustee at the time. As Michael Young he had been one of the first pupils of the original school and had become a prolific social entrepreneur, setting up amongst other things the Open University and later the University of the Third Age. He recommended that before the Trust established such a big scheme, market research should be carried out, and he offered to help us design the process. Questions were addressed to two groups: the sort of people who read *Resurgence* magazine; and a series of what would today be called Focus Groups, who also might be expected to understand the idea. In addition, we were asked to develop a business plan to put to the Trustee body.

Over several months the committee developed a detailed prospectus and worked out a course programme using the network of activists in the ecological movement, building on the contacts that Satish and Dartington had made over the years. In particular it was necessary to consider not only the underlying principles of the proposed college but its practical embodiment within a venue for learning. Satish brought his experience as a Jain monk and of the Gandhian movement in India. The school at Dartington had been influenced by Tagore from Leonard Elmhirst's time in India. With other inspirations, this is what came to shape aspects of the College design.

The results of the market research seemed to show that there was an interest in, and a thirst for, the type of programme proposed for the new College. The business plan put forward to the Trustees proved acceptable, and approval was given for the continued development of the project.

When recently asked to reflect on the creation of Schumacher College, John Pontin (Chairman of the Trustees at the time) remembers especially the enthusiasm of Satish Kumar. He also says that John Lane was enormously important in creating the climate among the Trustee body within which such a proposal could take root. He told me that once the idea of a Green University had been expressed to the Trustees, it never fell away as an idea. At that time the Trustees were burdened by the need for closures of various Estate activities, and inevitably they felt that instead of just closing things they wanted to start something worthwhile which would satisfy the Trust's educational objectives. At the same time they had to convince themselves and others that they were not irresponsibly indulging themselves on a whim in setting up another expensive project that would soon need to be closed.

Having made the commitment in October of 1989 to support the creation of Schumacher College, the Trustees carried forward their decision by allocating the Old Postern as its base. The Old Postern is a beautiful mediaeval manor house occupying a secluded site away from the centre of the Estate, and is a warren of comfortably sized interlinking rooms, some lit from above, which together create an inspirational space in which to live and learn. It had more than forty single bedrooms for student accommodation and had recently been used as a modest conference centre, so it was in reasonable repair. The Trustees endorsed substantial capital expenditure for the period 1990 to 1991 (£200,000) to ensure that the space met current statutory requirements in respect of fire precautions etc. They allocated funds for staff to be engaged in the autumn of 1990 to prepare for the opening of the College in January 1991.

For many people their recollection of this period is of an extended time of chaos and uncertainty. Actually, from the time of the first mention of the idea at the Trustee meetings in January 1989 to the opening of the College was just short of two years. I have always thought that for the creation of such a radical place this was surely not unduly lengthy.

Before the College's opening, the planning group worked through many aspects of College life, trying to establish the broad design of the curriculum and how it would be delivered. They considered certain key areas of College operations and made several decisions about the design before staff were recruited or the College opened. Woven through and deeply permeating the practical structures which supported the design, were the spiritual and ecological values implicit in the new paradigm. The governance of the College, its programme, decisions about the food and the staffing model were taken in the light of and to express this inspiration. Inevitably, after a couple of years there was a need to review what had been decided and make some modifications.

The governance of the College

As an activity of The Dartington Hall Trust the new College was technically a Department of the Trust. The Director of the College, initially Satish Kumar, would be responsible to the Trust and, at that time, control would be exercised on behalf of the Trustees through the Estate Council. (This was the new name for the modified Chairman's Group.) In practice, this line of supervision operated first through me as a member of the Estate Council and through John Lane who was its Chair.

In an effort to model participative and egalitarian principles, staff were not only to be paid broadly similar salaries but they were to work as a group of equals to manage the work of the College. Satish Kumar was the Director, and Brian Nicholson, who was to be resident at the Old Postern, was in effect its Administrator. At the time this seemed to be a clear mode of operation, but it didn't recognise on the one hand the emerging aspirations of members of the 'community' to manage and control their own affairs, or on the other, the absence of interest in the technical governance issue. This highlights the matter of how the Trust's hierarchical system of control played itself out in the face of the staff's more egalitarian intentions. It is explored in Chapter 10, where I list some of the challenges that faced the College.

The programme

From the beginning Schumacher College was concerned to study the ways in which the world was seen and understood at the end of the millennium. It aimed to explore alternative ways of understanding which were more holistic and resulted in actions which were less destructive to the Earth and to its inhabitants than those which had been legitimised as 'economic development' and 'progress'. The mainstream of industrial culture tended to view the world through the eyes of conventional reductionist science, and took a shallow consumer-oriented and materialistic economic view. The planning committee felt that these perspectives had captured the general imagination and the mainstream academic agenda, and permeated not only the academic institutions but also the media and the professions. It was our ambition to expose this incomplete and flawed worldview and to spend the larger part of College time in looking at alternative perspectives. The way the College was to be organised would also demonstrate that there were other possible ways of living which might avoid the despoliation of the planet brought about through the mainstream paradigm.

In summary, the programme in the first couple of years addressed aspects of the new science; it looked at psychological and spiritual issues, alternative economics, design, and assumptions behind the new paradigm. In the second year, ecophilosophy and an exploration of the great wisdom traditions were added. At the same time the College's first business courses looked at the transformation of economic life and thought, and explored how the dynamism of business could be harnessed to positive effect to help create an ecologically responsible vision for the world. Explorations of how some of the technological solutions applied to solve societal and political problems, have de-sacralised Nature and diminished the credibility of traditional systems of knowledge, were also introduced. All these themes have remained regular features of the College's programme.

Food

One of the crucial decisions made about the College, before it began, was that its food would be vegetarian. Initially this was a principled decision by the planning committee founded on the fact that the College should demonstrate that you could have a satisfying and enjoyable diet even if you did not eat meat. It was a belief based on the understanding that if everyone followed a vegetarian regime there would be enough food for everyone in the world and no-one need starve. We believed that if students were introduced to vegetarian food, they might begin to change their personal eating habits thus reducing their global footprint at the same time as helping improve the lot of the poorest on the planet.

This decision was reinforced by the local Food and Hygiene Officers, who said that if our students were to cook for each other, they could only work with vegetarian food. This was because fish and meat products carry with them the highest risks of contaminating food that is stored alongside. Since it was our intention that course participants would work together in the kitchens, and we saw cooking vegetarian food as part of their whole learning experience, we were happy to comply with this requirement.

As the years have passed it is interesting that emerging and wider ecological concerns have often first expressed themselves on the food agenda in the College, and food policies have developed to reflect this. In particular, it was the intention initially to buy, by preference, organic food if it was available. Sometimes this was difficult, and even when it was available it was usually much more expensive than conventionally produced food. Such expenditure was challenged as extravagant when the College was incurring substantial deficits. I defended it on the grounds that it was part of the curriculum, and this position was accepted by the Trust. With perseverance, we found that over time growers and sellers of local food began to appear. Much of their produce was organic or had low chemical inputs, and the price charged seemed more reasonable.

The issue of food miles was important from the beginning, so we always tried to purchase locally grown and seasonal food. This enabled the College to avoid purchases reliant on the use of fossil fuels in heated greenhouses and in expensive transportation. However, there were several problems with seasonal food. Our intentions for an exciting vegetarian diet would be difficult to realise with entirely locally grown seasonal produce. The students and staff, like everyone else, had their food preferences and addictions, and it soon became obvious that if they were not allowed to have their coffee or oranges and bananas, there might be revolution! People were invited to try alternatives, and aim to reduce their consumption of products which were not organically produced and which came from far away. The results of this strategy were some changes in dietary habits, and importantly it stimulated debate without using coercion. It was by this time (1994) that we began to search out fairly traded products such as coffee. One of the reservations we had about buying the conventional product was that the producers were being exploited and didn't get fairly paid for their work. This in turn had an effect on the environment as producers in what was then called the 'Third World' were forced out of business, and probably became part of the drift into the cities so that their traditional farming communities and habitats were destroyed.

Later the subject of genetically modified (GM) foods emerged as an issue. One of the staff at the time was Professor Brian Goodwin,[17] who became a central figure in a national group of scientists aiming to draw the attention of the government to the potential problems of GM technology. We also had on staff activists who were fighting the introduction of GM crops in the locality. The staff body agreed that it did not want such foods at the College, and Julia Ponsonby[18] who was then in charge of catering, took on the task of identifying whether the ingredients of any of the manufactured products bought, such as pasta, contained GM ingredients. This involved much correspondence and eventually letters to say that if we could not be certain that a particular supplier's goods were free of GMOs, then we would be taking our business elsewhere. I believe that this action on Julia's part was important in establishing the principle of labelling to help with identification of GMOs. Certainly, it was not too long before such communication with suppliers became less necessary.

Communal work

An important ecological principle is that of relationship. We are who we are, in part because of our relationships with others. Recognising this, one of the intentions of the planning committee was to create dense webs of relationships between all the people in the College. It was also decided there should not be a servant class in the College, and that domestic tasks would be carried out through a work group system. The process would build on the inherent educational opportunities and was managed to some extent by selecting the membership of the small work groups before students arrived. The pattern of work group activity was to ensure that people were involved, usually with staff, in as much significant communal activity as possible. The practice gave an introduction, to some for the first time, to 'the work of the world' and to the satisfaction of seeing it well done. (In a poem by Marge Piercy that was often read at Morning Meetings she says, 'the thing worth doing, well done has a shape that satisfies, clean and evident'). It also quickly made people feel at home because they felt essential to the life of the place. Further, it established that a servant body was not necessary to service the needs of the 'more important' academic endeavour.

Permanent staffing

It was clear to the original planning committee that all the academic, domestic and pastoral aspects of the College agenda could not be delivered by a visiting academic faculty. The Trust therefore provided sufficient funds to recruit a core faculty who would be both permanent and in residence, and be appointed in time to help plan the new College. In addition to their particular expertise, they would have a clear commitment to new paradigm thinking, and would be willing to share with students all the communal tasks necessary for the smooth running of the College.

In order to probe the work of visiting scholars-in-residence, the core staff between them needed to be able to examine how the development of Western scientific and rational thought influences how we see the world. They had to understand the individual's psychological and cognitive processes in creating the global crisis. It was important that a scientific ecological perspective was represented. In addition, and at an equivalent level in the College, someone was needed to plan and enable the community to prepare a wholesome vegetarian diet. Further, it was recognised that an artist must be included to promote the place of the imagination and creativity in the College.

The original team included Satish Kumar and Brian Nicholson. Newly recruited were Helen Challoner (to manage the food provision), Guy Claxton (an educational psychologist), Stephan Harding (a scientific ecologist) and Karen Thomas, who had recently completed her arts studies at Dartington College.

Scholars-in-Residence

Early on in the planning it was decided to call the key visiting teachers 'Scholars-in-Residence'. This communicated the intentions about their role. They were called 'scholars' because it was the expectation that they would still be probing the roots of their own field of study. They were 'in residence' because they were expected to live at the College for an extended period of time and pursue their thinking with the resident students as well as to hold classes. The people who first agreed to come to the College for this experimental programme of courses reflected the focus we intended to place on the studies. They were all eminent in the green movement, and many had been to Dartington during the time of the Education Conferences. The programming group believed that those invited were living out the implications of the ecological worldview in their own lives and work.

Some people in the green movement were keen that there should be a place where the examination of the new paradigm could begin, and many were willing to support such work by coming to teach. The planning group had several criteria in their selection. First, they should have a clear intellectual understanding of their material and have communicated it through their books. Secondly, they had to be able to make an impact on their listeners through lectures; they had to be able to convince or make sense to both the 'converted' and the unconvinced; and not least they needed to embody their teachings in their own lives. In addition, they should be activists. Since the ecological movement and individuals in it often lacked a platform from which to teach in depth, it was the intention that the College would provide this. It was our hope that students would come and be inspired by these teachers to become agents for ecological change in the world.

Exactly who were the people who were willing to come to the College for up to five weeks to lead these initial courses? What characteristics, if any, did they share? What has happened to them subsequently? Certainly most of them have achieved recognition of their work and some have received international awards, such as the 'Right Livelihood Award', sometimes called 'The Alternative Nobel Prize'. Some had given a Schumacher Lecture, an annual event hosted here in the UK by the Schumacher Society. Most of them were lone individuals following their personal journey without the security (or constraints) of paid employment or tenure in an academic institution. It was also important that women were recruited to teach, and that we had teachers who would offer a non-Eurocentric perspective of the world. It was not always easy to satisfy all these requirements, but this remained our ambition. And as the years progressed, we eventually realised that some people used our list of teachers to guide their reading and deepen their knowledge of the new paradigm!

Students

"They are the persons who will carry a spark of sincerely devoted intelligence into the dark nights of the planet." – James Hillman (Scholar-in-Residence)

It was important to have a vision of the students we wanted to attract in order to help the recruitment process and inform the design of the College. Originally the intention had been to attract adults from anywhere in the world who had a deep interest in the curriculum on offer. In the original planning it had been decided not to offer accreditation, because we wanted an environment where the investigations could follow whatever directions emerged, and to be free of the constraining influence of a prescribed syllabus. Broadly, our hope was to attract as students those willing to spend a significant period of time (in our first programmes, our courses were five weeks long) in exploring and uncovering the roots of the current worldview and in developing a critical understanding of its limitations. Together they would examine how the current mainstream paradigm could be modified through the application of ecological principles and spiritual values. Our ambition that students should come from all walks of life and all parts of the world was realised from the very beginning: in the first year we welcomed students of all ages and professional backgrounds from forty-five countries. To support these students, bursary funds (largely from The Dartington Hall Trust but also from other philanthropists) had been raised, and this had funded the full costs of attendance on each course for as many as five or six good students from poorer economic backgrounds. This number represented up to 20% of each course group, with the advantage that a wide cross-section of the global community could be represented, thus enhancing the diversity and quality of the resulting debate.

On application forms, potential students were asked to describe their occupations. Regardless of age, many still described themselves as students: others were teachers, often at universities, but sometimes of young children. Over the years it was also evident that many worked in the helping professions and a considerable number were in religious orders. There were also designers of various kinds, from architects to landscape gardeners, and individual entrepreneurs and business people. A person describing herself as 'a newly single grandmother' represented a whole group at significant turning points in their lives. In addition there were people searching for the direction of a second career, and others who used the College as a place where they could come over several years to follow a programme of self-development. The majority of students were in their late thirties and older: a small minority were in their twenties, and a similarly small number in their seventies and eighties. We soon recognised that it was a mature twenty-year-old who was drawn to come to the College, but those who were proved to be truly exceptional, and have often made a real difference in the world. They had leadership qualities, and often became catalysts of change in their home communities.

In the first year nine courses were offered, and just short of 200 students came. They came from as far away as Australia, Brazil, India and the USA. From Africa we had students from Zambia and Zimbabwe. They also came from Western and Eastern Europe, Scandinavia and Russia. Slightly over 50% were women. Generally speaking, the same pattern of age and gender has continued, with enrolment being largely influenced by the subjects of study and the reputation of the teachers. Economics courses almost always attract more men, and psychology courses seem to bring more women.

After ten years the figures showed, not surprisingly, that this trend had continued, and that half the students had come from the UK; they outnumbered the next largest groups three times. The next largest categories came in almost equal numbers from North America and Western Europe, then Eastern Europe, with smaller numbers from the rest of the world. Despite having some funds available and the will to accept students from Africa, it was very difficult to get them here. It seemed that the problem probably lay with immigration controls in the U.K.

Whatever their origins, the students have been outstanding. David Orr,[19] one of the College's regular teachers whose work focuses on ecoliteracy, said in a recent letter, "The College has attracted some of the most extraordinary students I've had the privilege to know. The alumni list of those students increasingly reads like a Who's Who? in numerous fields. I've run into former Schumacher students in some very important places."

Focal points

- There needs to be a commitment to detailed planning if an idea is to be translated into concrete form. Because of the risks of disappointment or failure there are costs, both financial and psychological, for both those who fund and those who carry out the planning. A group with diverse skills is necessary to carry out the research and make the required preparations.
- Nevertheless, planning is a vital part of the development process because exposing the ideas to detailed scrutiny refines them and builds understanding between members of the group. It also raises and enhances support for the project as the 'market' is tested and the findings are incorporated. The end of the process should reveal a sounder proposal than the original idea.

Chapter 5

Creating the context: the hidden curriculum

In dwelling be close to the land.
In meditation go deep in the heart.
In dealing with others, be gentle and kind.
In speech, be true.
In ruling, be just.
In business, be competent.
In action, watch the timing.

– Lao Tsu

The College, then, was to have two aspects to the curriculum. The first was displayed in the programme of courses and was represented by the people who had been invited to teach them. The second part was the 'hidden curriculum', where the processes of living together were arranged so that the ecological and spiritual values that were being explored in each course should be lived out in the daily routines of College life.

This hidden curriculum was itself in two parts. On the one hand, the College adopted certain practices or routines and processes including the daily timetable, which have subsequently been described as the Schumacher educational model. On the other, the physical space was carefully arranged and decorated.

Part One: the daily practices

One area discussed in detail before the College opened, and subsequently refined in the light of experience, was the daily timetable. It is the most obvious aspect of the Schumacher model. It was vital that the College create and hold a context for the daily activities. We planned and there evolved a regular pattern which incorporated ritual and routine, silence and meditation, freedom to spend time as one wished, safety in which to listen to and challenge the teachers, privacy for reflection or recreation, community work and communal celebration. There was always a risk that in their eagerness to learn as much as possible in a short visit to the College, some individuals were not able to establish a healthy balance between work and 'digestion' of their learning. Partly for this reason, weekends on the longer courses were left largely free so that students could spend the time individually or in small groups without external expectations or demands. It was hoped that this freedom would enable people to explore the area and take some organised trips – for example to the Eden Project in Cornwall, walks on Dartmoor, bike rides down to Dartmouth, or lazy days in Totnes digesting their learning.

On their arrival, new students would familiarise themselves with each other and with the place. In the evening of the first full day there was usually a game to help people learn each other's names. Also on this first evening the facilitator worked with the course participants to agree the daily programme for the course. Students wanted to know the schedule as soon as possible. They felt then that they had been given the power to influence what was going to happen and understood that this probably meant they might have some control over how the rest of the course developed. The regular routines provided students with a sense of security and eliminated a significant potential source of anxiety.

Essentially, therefore, the College day was divided into several sections: it began with reflection, meditation and setting the tone for the day, followed by physical activity. The mornings were intended to provide intellectual stimulus and food for thought, whilst the afternoons were intended to be opportunities to reflect on and digest this input. Field trips and creative work in the afternoons were programmed both for their own sake and also to encourage digestion of the learning. Small group tutorials before supper with the Scholar-in-Residence created a space to reflect together on the learning, be it purely cerebral, spiritual or aesthetic. Evenings were rather more concerned with students finding out about each other's life and work, and were designed to build the relationships which would carry forward after students left the College and returned to their normal lives. Encouragement was given for individuals to take time out of the schedule as needed in order to get sufficient exercise or personal space.

THE BASIC TIMETABLE

0715   Meditation
0800   Breakfast
0830   Morning Meeting followed by communal work with staff
0930   Break
1000   Morning classes
Coffee break
1300   Lunch followed by clear-up
1415   Field trip, free time, study groups
1600   Tea
1630   Supper preparation by one work group
1700   Academic tutorial with Scholar-in-Residence
1800   Optional Meditation
1830   Supper followed by clear-up
2000   Evening sessions: for example,
        Satish's fireside chat
        Participant presentations
        Open evening
        Celebrations / Soirée
Later: Free time, perhaps in the bar

The College found that the predictability of the routine timetable was liberating for many students, and it provided something to rail against for those who did not find it so! It was through the punctuation of the day with regular work groups that people sometimes had their first recognition of ecological cycles. It was whilst carrying out the communal chores, meeting the staff whom they would not otherwise see, that they often learnt something unexpected – usually something they didn't know they wanted to know! And importantly, if the Scholar-in-Residence (as occasionally happened) was unable to come or became ill during their visit, there was a framework within which an alternative programme could be devised. For many, such a routine was transformative and offered an insight into a reflective and meditative way of life, which they carried back home and incorporated into previously frenetic lives.

It has been my experience that in the same way as some people can be greedy with their food, there may be a similar greed for intellectual nour-ishment. If offered the chance to hear or talk more about what interested them, some will indulge themselves until an outside observer might feel they needed some time for digestion! It was partly to counter this tendency that the day was designed with periods for reflection and quietness as well as sessions for meditation. Whilst we never insisted that everyone attended meditation, course participants were invited to try it out. Some non-denominational instruction was offered so that the inexperienced could see if they found such spiritual practice rewarding.

To implement the Schumacher model, staff had to be able to help each new group learn, and when carrying out the communal work, be willing to engage with each student if necessary. All staff needed to understand the importance of the community working together, and some needed to be able to lead small cooking groups in the afternoons, where not only was the evening meal prepared but conversations took place about, for example, the classes of the day, the issue of food miles, why at the College there is a veg-etarian diet, or about the personal lives and work of the group members.

In short, it was intended that there should be congruence between the taught curriculum and the practices of the College. It seemed obvious to the planning group that the physical arrangements of the place would also communicate some kind of message, and we wanted to ensure that it was an ecological and spiritual one.

Part Two: The physical arrangements

People learn as much from the environment in which they are studying as from their teachers and indeed fellow students. Some of this learning is conscious, but it can also be – and often is – unconscious. Unless it is drawn to their attention, some course participants just don't notice what they are learning. This is the reason that in Schumacher College each group works at intervals during their stay with a member of staff to reflect on what is being learned and how it is being learned.

In order to ensure that the messages students take from the College environment reinforce the learning agenda, we paid attention to the cre-ation of a space which set the tone for ecological and spiritual study. Where possible, the selection of furnishings and decorations was made to create a context for the style of study we intended to promote.

The College as a whole was seen to be an aspect of the curriculum. We recognised that learning can take place everywhere, not least in the kitchen, the dining room and other functional spaces; it can also take place – and can do so subliminally – in the overall atmosphere, spirit and mood of the course. The colour of the walls, the design of the furniture, the choice of fabrics, the quality of the organisation, the care paid to the preparation and the serving of its food, the courtesies of its staff – all these should be graced by unity, harmony, imagination and simplicity; all these are aspects of an overall concern for the spirit of its visitors. Education through aesthetics can be as important as book learning and Socratic dialogue.

We considered that a beautiful environment is an essential and integral element of any true education. We can absorb all kinds of information, but if we do so in an ugly environment, the ugliness can distort the quality of our learning. Almost subliminally we will absorb coarseness, stridency and a lack of harmony, and our learning will have been negatively influenced. We therefore took care within a fairly tight budget to make the rooms as beautiful and graceful as possible.

Over the years many students have remarked upon the beauty and the quiet and calm of the building. Yet it has been a constant challenge to maintain this atmosphere, especially as people have wanted to gift works to the College. Commonly there has been a desire to introduce electronic music into the workspaces. Perhaps this was to make people feel even more at home! My sense was that such aural 'wallpapering' detracted from the environment of mindfulness and calm we had intended. In my years at the College I must have upset many people who couldn't understand my apparent preference for silence to their choice of music.

It became recognised practice at the end of each course to strip the space back to its original furnishings. It was important not to do this too soon – i.e. before the course participants left – so that they didn't feel that 'their space' was being destroyed. Equally, it was important that the messages and atmosphere of any group did not maintain a permanent hold on the feel of the College. The language that we used to describe and help people understand this, was that we took care to create a 'new vessel' within which learning could take place afresh by each new group. Within this space, new course participants could to some extent create their own atmosphere, but, with guidance from the staff, we encouraged them to understand the place would be returned to its essentials when they left. There were some exceptions to this. I remember we had a helper who, one autumn, collected fallen leaves from the Dartington Hall Gardens – beautiful red maple leaves. She dried them and threaded them on fine cotton, and made a hanging of these 'falling leaves' which graced the main hall for several years.

Modelling ecological practices

Through the design of the day and the design of the place it was possible to set a certain tone, but there were some aspects of the College where it was difficult to directly show what such a building would be like in an ecologically conscious age. One example was in the field of energy conservation. Schumacher College was set up in an old country house which was mediaeval in its foundations. In the simple sense of its survival, in parts, for five centuries, it certainly is demonstrably sustainable. In other respects, such as in its use of energy, it is extravagant. To take just one example, some of its present windows in the main building were placed there during a refurbishment in the early twentieth century when the Elmhirsts acquired it for their home. Since then the building has been 'listed' as being of considerable architectural importance, and current regulations do not permit us to alter the windows significantly. Best practice in energy conservation is therefore limited to hanging thick, insulating curtains. From a practical point of view we need to maintain good ventilation, so we could not simply put secondary glazing inside the windows. We therefore use the situation as an example of the constraints people have to work within whilst still addressing the issue of energy efficiency. In our case, course participants are reminded to take action themselves to close the windows and draw the curtains as night falls and the cold tries to creep in.

The situation with the windows in the residential accommodation built in the 1970s is rather different. In 1994, looking to upgrade our energy efficiency, we established that the windows are so small that the heat loss they cause is relatively low as compared with the potential loss through the walls or roof. At that time therefore it was more ecologically sound and much cheaper to upgrade the cavity wall and loft insulation than to expensively double-glaze the whole accommodation buildings, so this was what we did. In almost all courses someone would mention the absence of double or secondary glazing, and this would provide a useful discussion point enabling students to reflect on such issues in their own lives. What it really required was that the staff of the College were confident enough to engage students in conversation about these shortcomings rather than feel defensive or unable to use the situation creatively. Discussions of such matters at the regular staff meetings were partly intended to educate staff about the complexity of such issues so they could discuss them with students when the matters arose.

Management style of the College

The management style can be thought of as the expression of the values and spirit which underpin the College's work. It is through the processes of management that the daily experience of everyone in the College is created, maintained and fine-tuned. 'Management style' describes not only the personal practices of the Director, but includes how everyone involved in running the College implements the spirit expressed in the general principles listed below. It is vital that the way the College is managed chimes with the educational principles it espouses. Over time, these principles have evolved as a guide to the daily running of the College. As all staff and helpers have a facilitation role with regard to the course participants, everyone is expected to act in the light of these principles.

THE PRINCIPLES BY WHICH THE COLLEGE RUNS

The College's purpose is to provide inspiration to its students through the visiting teachers, through its staff, and by the way the College itself reflects ecological and spiritual values.

The College is an educational establishment aiming to bring out the best in its students and staff. It aims to create opportunities for discovery by each individual. It also starts from the assumption that any individual, whether staff or student, behaves with the best of intentions. This might sound naive, and indeed sometimes (though rarely) this assumption proved ill-founded.

To demonstrate its agenda, the College's practices must respect the immediate environment, Nature, and the wider world.

(continued overleaf)

THE PRINCIPLES BY WHICH THE COLLEGE RUNS
(continued)

Not simply because it is an important educational principle, but because an ethical dimension is integral to the ecological and spiritual worldview, respect and compassion should be shown for all, whether humans or other–than-humans.

Rules and hierarchy must be minimised in College systems and be replaced by a general principle that people should treat others as they themselves would like to be treated. Sometimes people found this difficult to comprehend, and requested more specific rules to live by. On occasion particular groups instituted new rules, for example about saying Grace before meals, but almost without exception such practices would lapse.

Staff should aim to devolve responsibility to students as much as possible to illustrate, and allow everyone to experience, the emergence of co-responsibility.

To enable people to enjoy the experience of living in community, staff need to remember that the students are fully autonomous adults to be encouraged rather than compelled or coerced to carry out the community work.

In the life of the College, the tension and balance must be held between the needs of any individual and those of the group; between each person's rights and their responsibilities; between individual freedom and the constraints imposed to protect community integrity; between routine and flexibility; between work and play, and between intellectual, creative and physical work.

The College must provide an opportunity for all members of the community to give service to colleagues, to the students and the whole community.

In order to demonstrate the value of all kinds of work, staff and students need to take their part in all necessary community work.

Through its practices the College should attempt to demonstrate ecological good-practice, for example through recycling, reducing its use of resources, reusing where possible, through its purchasing policies of both capital items and its more regular purchase of smaller items like food, paper and cleaning products.

Student reaction

The response of students to the way the College is managed, and the way it applies these principles, varies according to the individual's personality. Some individuals see a self-organising community with emergent properties, leading to the creation of effective learning groups. Others see a puppet-master pulling the strings to contrive a particular learning experience for each group. Others don't give the matter any consideration, and give themselves over to enjoying it. A similar divergence is clear in attitudes to authority, staff roles and the perception of hierarchies and privilege. Some expect or even want what they call clear management, others might prefer a little less clarity and even more ambiguity, and yet others want a hands-off style. Some want the staff to be friends, whilst others prefer more remote figures. And of course the individual staff have their own preferred ways of being.

These differences play themselves out in the attitude to rules. My preference was always to ask everyone to treat others as they would wish to be treated themselves. One of the strongest expectations is that everyone fulfils their community responsibilities. For some this is sufficient, or even too much guidance, but others want more specificity. Some people want to introduce new rules, and there is sufficient flexibility within the system to allow an individual to try to persuade others of the efficacy of their newly proposed rule. Almost always, in the process of persuasion, the benefits of flexibility emerge as preferable to rigid rules, and eventually people seem to lose interest in introducing new rules. For new students the absence of rules is sometimes a joy and for others it is a source of anxiety, but by the end of a course there always seems to have emerged a level of comfort with assuming responsibility for one's own behaviour and with taking care of others.

The staff role

Primarily it is important that regardless of their particular role, staff remember to help course participants to learn. It requires that staff understand the work so they can model the ecological and spiritual principles by which the College runs. This provides challenges for us all, since none of us has perfect ecological credentials! Some fly around the world in search of the sun, others find it impossible to resist the temptation to eat foods out of season: yet others find it difficult to be less than strident in criticism of others' work choices, or their ecologically damaging lifestyles. Much of this is to do with making judgements about others, so we have to remind ourselves to be non-judgemental about College guests and about each other. Instead we have to trust that the context of the place is powerful enough to guide people to make their own self-evaluations.

It became accepted over time that as a staff group, in day-to-day matters we need to model co-operative and egalitarian working methods. By our actions we have to demonstrate that we are taking care of our colleagues and the cyclical tasks associated with life in a community. Regardless of our job description, each of us has to do what needs to be done and not leave community work for 'someone else' to do. Visitors soon notice this, even if they haven't registered that there isn't a servant body to care for their needs. Given the policy of encouraging rather than forcing the students to learn, it is intended that each new person is able to learn in his or her own way. Inevitably, student learning involves forgetfulness and neglect of responsibilities until they register the consequences of their actions. It is then that they do what is required because they understand why it is necessary. Sometimes, of course, they don't do what is required because they haven't understood (or pretend they haven't understood) why it is necessary, and someone else has to pick up the pieces!

Day-to-day decision-making

Whenever unprecedented circumstances arise, it is important that they are evaluated against our general principles. For example, an intention is that we will, in our actions, tread lightly on the Earth. This applies to questions about what to do in the garden, what new chairs to buy, and whether to buy soya milk in tetra paks, or make it in-house. Having made a decision, it could quickly be altered as circumstances changed, if as a staff body we had consciously reasoned through our thinking in the first place.

Another dimension of the College's co-operative working is that consultation with the wider College community is encouraged before an individual takes unilateral action. Some people said they found that this approach stifled their creativity. My sense is that the involvement of the whole group (though often only the staff and current helper group, it has to be said) ensures that decision-making is better informed and that important information is not overlooked. Staff could also present the views of absentees or, ideally, time could be allowed so that other voices could be sought. It is an important part of the process of keeping everyone informed and feeling involved. As people learn the factors behind how and why decisions are made, it actually assists the process in other areas, especially at those times where key responsible staff are not present.

Essentially, it is the intention that when unprecedented circumstances arise there is a general understanding of how they might be managed. There is a shared understanding that most issues could be discussed by the staff and student bodies. Where decisions need to be made instantly, it is agreed that the person on the ground faced with the problem could make a decision in the spirit of the College as they understand it. It is also agreed that such decisions may need to be reversed by management. With issues of less urgency there can be a more protracted process. Such issues were brought to the daily staff meeting for consideration, where they would be discussed often over an extended period, until an agreement was reached, or interest was lost. This would apply for example, to questions about what to do in the garden or how to manage College Open Evenings.

Helpers / volunteer staff

Voluntary roles for people to help run the College emerged in the first year. There had been no intention to design such an opportunity into the staffing, but gradually a small (four or five) and changing group of volunteers assumed an important part in its running. David Cadman[20] has been here as a student, on retreat, and a couple of times as a teacher but, he says, for him best of all was to be a helper working with, and learning from, the rhythm and depth of the daily life. It was a symbiotic relationship, illustrating a mutually beneficial arrangement. The selected ex-student was able to live at the College for a limited period, sometimes as little as a month, and use its resources. In return, the College could call on his or her services for sixteen hours a week to help with routine tasks and, as importantly, to support the resident student population. Helpers would have learned about the College during their course of study, and staff would have had a chance to get to know them. In general, helpers staying for relatively short periods were very happy with the system. Those staying for a long time, even up to a year, sometimes began to feel exploited and wanted to design for themselves a more permanent role. In practice, what sometimes happened was that long-term volunteers applied to fill staff vacancies. For the College a fine balance had to be struck between on the one hand offering an opportunity for service, and on the other hand viewing helpers as free labour, and thus becoming over-dependent on the generosity of the volunteers.

After the review in 1993, the original staffing model – where the core faculty together ran the College – was replaced. In addition to an overall Director (Anne Phillips), there was a Director of Programmes (Satish Kumar) and one key academic (Stephan Harding) representing the central ecological focus of the work. The rest of the staff body was largely, though not entirely, administrative and service staff. At the same time it was made explicit that the helpers were important (if voluntary) members of the staff group, and that they should attend the daily staff meetings.

Staff meetings

As part of the regular running of the College, it was daily practice to meet as a staff group each morning at coffee time. Partly social and recreational, it was also a time to reflect on the progress of the current course, or deal with any immediate matters. Staff could think about how and whether they needed to modify their own work in relation to the current group, thus making it easier to weave the course requirements into the normal College operations. For example, a visiting teacher might suddenly ask to take the group out on an unusual field trip. If staff had been alerted to the possibility, they could anticipate the consequences and make preparations to accommodate the trip. The occasion also served as a time to introduce new staff and helpers to the ways the College worked, as they listened to the exchanges over the issues of the day.

As the College matured and activity levels increased, it was decided that a separate meeting of the permanent staff was needed to discuss issues of substance. Some items, such as certain helper issues or how staff were carrying out their duties, were perhaps best discussed without helpers present. Other items had implications beyond the 'lifetime' of a normal helper, and permanent staff imagined they would not be concerned. It also seemed that discussing matters with just the permanent staff could be more efficient since a deeper overall knowledge of the College's work could be assumed. Despite the benefits of this practice, it became clear that it had the potential to cause difficulties since some helpers, having had the expectation of being fully involved, felt excluded.

Nevertheless, through these various processes individual members of staff acquired the skills to support the students on their personal learning journeys. There are numerous examples of students arriving with a vague question about what to do with the rest of their lives, and leaving with a much clearer picture of a future in which their own contribution had taken on a sharper focus. Often this came not from the formal course teacher but through the informal conversations and discussions, sometimes in the small hours, and especially with helpers who seemed to have the stamina to stay up late. Helpers remember their own experiences when they originally came to the College wondering how they might make a contribution to resolving the crisis that faces us in the world today. This informal provision of support to the learners is a crucial role for the helpers. Full-time staff have responsibilities, personal or work-related, which mean that they have limited time to be available for the course participants 'out of hours'. Yet it is an important feature of the College that this support is provided.

Focal points

- Having grasped the intellectual framework of, in our case, the ecological and spiritual paradigm, the subject matter of the courses and the selection of the teachers becomes apparent.
- It would be possible to attempt to teach using the traditional methods of mainstream academia. However,
- Schumacher College approached the learning process holistically with the intention that the daily activities, the surroundings and the College's practices reinforced the focus of the courses and provided the opportunity for their implications to be explored in the College environment.

Chapter 6

The evolution of policy

"Schumacher College is just what our world needs now – an opportunity for people from diverse cultures to meet in a welcoming, beautiful learning environment with our planet's practical visionaries. To be with people seeking to deepen and clarify their life paths is uplifting."

– Frances Moore Lappé, Scholar-in-Residence 2002

The original planning group did not, of course, take a view on all aspects of how the College would operate. In some cases it is only by dealing with the same issues time and again that a policy gradually evolves. Applying general principles of compassion, considering our relationship with the planet and with each other, realising our interdependence and perhaps most particularly, remembering our learning agenda, an appropriate response to a given situation will emerge and, in due course, become policy. One such issue was in the area of individual dietary or other needs. Another one was the garden.

Dealing with students' special requirements

As time went on it became clear that an increasing number of students came with food allergies and dietary preferences. This should not have surprised us. First, people are recognising that it is often their food which is the source of their ill-health. Secondly, it is after studying modern farming and food production methods that they decide they need to investigate these ecological issues and they sometimes come to Schumacher College to find out more. Our practice of treating everyone with respect and compassion resulted in the policy of providing these individuals with the food which satisfied their needs, as long as it did not involve us in providing non-vegetarian food.

Since everyone is involved in the cooking rota, such needs open up a learning opportunity in the cooking groups. I remember one evening cooking shift where the small work group was cooking for about thirty people, both staff and students. Not only did we prepare the standard vegetarian option but also variations for vegans (non-dairy), for people who wouldn't eat cooked onions, and someone else who wouldn't eat raw onions or garlic in any form. Others wouldn't have peppers, and others were averse to mushrooms. Then there was the lady who was allergic only to eggs. Catering for that group of only thirty people was a real challenge.

Not many groups have such a diversity of dietary needs. Perhaps most common was the allergy to wheat, where we tried to encourage people to try spelt flour: more ancient and less refined, it causes fewer allergic reactions. People are encouraged to take responsibility for their own food needs, and if they aren't satisfied with what they are provided with, to cook for themselves. This is easier than it may sound, because students quickly become familiar with the kitchens as a result of the way the community work of the College is handled. This accommodation of an individual's dietary needs is deeply significant, especially as people with special needs may feel ignored or marginalised. Such individuals certainly come fearing that they will be ignored, and are delighted to find such care and respect.

Many students arrive at the College with anxieties not about their diet, but about other personal matters. People coming from Africa for the first time may be concerned about the cold. Language is another problem: some students spend much of the first week struggling to improve their fluency and experience the sheer exhaustion of listening to complex ideas expressed in a foreign tongue. People who are hard of hearing and sometimes trying to recognise unfamiliar accents need ongoing support if they are to achieve their ambitions. It is important that everyone's needs are met if the group is to be happy and run smoothly. Sometimes an individual might suddenly develop a severe cold or a migraine. This might be because of the stress of being in a completely new and demanding environment; also, since the students usually come on planes from all over the world, they often bring with them strange bugs. Being unwell, they may feel frightened and alone. Those students who have personal anxieties, whatever they might be, must be supported by staff and helpers so they can relax and learn with ease.

Taking care of the garden

Early in the life of the College it soon became clear the gardens would need a management policy. It was certainly an area of contention, and students often questioned why an ecological College didn't produce its own food. Whilst the garden area seems quite large compared with the average domestic plot, at just over an acre it is nowhere near large enough to produce enough to satisfy the College's need for any of its staple foods. The location in the south of England means that anything that is grown is usually ready for harvesting in late July and August – a time when the College is not in session and there is no-one in residence to enjoy it. The gardens can't satisfy the appetites of an average weekly resident population as high as fifty. All we can produce is small quantities of things like herbs to garnish our meals, or sometimes harvest enough rhubarb to provide a crumble everyone can taste.

Different interest groups have their own aspirations for the College garden. For example, representatives of The Dartington Hall Trust, which provides the largest part of the funding for the College, requested that we keep the boundaries of our land 'tidy' and in harmony with the larger Estate. This was at odds with the views of Stephan Harding, the College Ecologist,[21] who felt that while the trimmed yew trees might fit with the formal gardens of the Estate, they weren't ecological. He was also keen to leave certain areas to encourage wildlife by increasing the amount of nettles and brambles. He had led the planting of extensive areas of the College grounds with trees which acted as a shelter belt against the predominant south-westerly winds, and planted many trees elsewhere on the Estate. There was yet another group who wanted to play volleyball, and on some courses (e.g. Fritjof Capra's) it became traditional to have a volleyball tournament. At other times, helpers wanted to build ponds or create permaculture gardens.

All these different demands were balanced (not to everyone's satisfaction, it has to be admitted) by dividing the different areas of the grounds into different usages. Parts of the gardens retained their formality and commonality with gardens elsewhere on the Estate. Other parts were designated as recreational space, and the grass was regularly clipped for football and volleyball pitches. Some of the garden was set aside for horticultural experiments, and this seemed to work if there was a helper on staff who wished to take responsibility for the project for an extended period. The most successful project, which started from scratch, was the herb garden: its products were often added to the students' evening culinary experiments, and its flowers were cut to decorate the tables. (Needless to say, there were some who opposed the cutting of flowers simply for decoration, and there was often a lively debate about what the flowers really wanted. Normally compromises were reached in which most people's views were somehow accommodated (or perhaps people just gave up, deciding that some battles were not worth fighting!)

There were numerous new garden projects initiated by passing students. They started off looking wonderful and promising luscious delicacies for us all, but most disappeared under the prolific Devon weeds. Nevertheless, there remained areas where enthusiastic gardening participants could find a place to exercise their ambitions without upsetting anyone, and they were able to leave feeling that they had made a worthwhile long-term contribution to the College. Through these processes we acquired over the years an extensive area of rich wilderness, the volleyball area, the kitchen herb garden, an improved vegetable patch, some fruit and beautiful decorative trees.

In the absence of funds to employ a gardener, the knowledge of the gardens was held in the collective mind of the College staff/helper body. Whilst over the years the garden gradually improved, the staff learnt that we shouldn't 'bite off more than we could chew'. In terms of gardening projects, we had to select only those which could be maintained on a permanent basis without a dedicated gardener.

It was a part of our work which would have repaid investment, and after my time funds were made available by the Trust for the College to develop the educational potential of the gardens.

Focal points

- There is no substitute for scrupulous detailed explorations to reveal the opportunities and possible flaws within a project.
- Despite any amount of advance work it is certain that there will be unexpected outcomes and you should expect to have to respond to emerging challenges.
- The original design may have to be refined in accordance with the core principles which will have become clearer with the passage of time.
- Likewise, there may be pressures to expand, or include related activities, before the time is right. So, recognise your limitations and set boundaries to what your project can realistically achieve.

Chapter 7

Refining the model

This is what you should do; Love the earth and the sun and animals,
Despise riches, give alms to everyone who asks,
Stand up for the stupid and crazy,
Devote your income and labour to others, hate tyrants,
Argue not concerning God,
Have patience and indulgence toward the people,
Re-examine all you have been told in school or church or any book,
Dismiss what insults your very soul,
And your flesh shall become a great poem.

– Walt Whitman

A couple of years after the College opened it was apparent that the time had come for a root-and-branch review of the College's work. Financial concerns were perhaps the immediate trigger, but there were other questions about recruitment, governance, the learning model and the breadth of the curriculum. An extended process thus began, involving not only Dartington staff but also a small group of former participants eager to share their experience as facilitators to help the College move into its next phase.

In the first courses it was clear that the students had come to study with the leading thinkers. Despite the publicity material flagging up the intention to probe the ideas the scholars-in-residence were proposing, few students were inclined to treat very seriously the efforts of the core staff to do this. The core staff's initial excitement turned to demoralisation as their efforts were thwarted. Having balanced the day's activities between the intellectual input from the scholars and the practical community work, there seemed little time for further cerebral work. There was a body of opinion that skilled facilitators were needed to ensure that students learned most effectively, and as numbers attending the courses seemed to decline rather than grow, the design of the curriculum and the marketing model was also called into question. Whether it was realistic to retain the original staffing arrangements became the focus of sustained debate, and eventually a new model was adopted.

It was agreed that to a large extent staff were to have more of a supportive than a teaching function. They were to service the residential needs of the students and visiting teachers, and carry out the administrative functions of the College rather than be part of a teaching faculty. This then necessitated a new model of management for the College, and a different pattern for day-to-day supervision of the staff. In addition, the College's practices were to be reviewed and modified where appropriate in order to enhance the learning environment.

When the College was first set up it was thought that five weeks was the shortest time needed to cover the planned intellectual material and allow for the anticipated personal transformations. After this review, the length of the courses was reduced to three weeks to enlarge the pool of people from which to recruit and thus make the College more accessible. It was felt that anything shorter would be neither effective nor manageable. During the first of the three weeks, the level of staff input was high as new arrivals were introduced to the systems and structures in the College. Week two was somewhat easier, as students generally by then understood how things worked and this reduced the pressure on staff. Week three coasted down to the last minute endings and preparations for the next arrivals. Staff found this model sustainable and manageable, whilst course participants confirmed the effectiveness of the three-week model if they were to really learn what the College had to teach.

The new organisational model

Governance

It was at this time that I was appointed Director. I was based at the College full-time, and managed day-to-day matters. The Trust created a Supervisory Group to oversee the work of the College, to which the Director reported each term. Membership of this Supervisory Group included John Lane (as a representative Trustee), Satish Kumar, the Director of Programmes, myself as Director and Ivor Stolliday, the Trust's senior executive at the time. John Lane has said that if there had been any major concerns about the College, it would have been the job of this group to flag them to the Trustees and he had every confidence that it would have done so.

The Director's responsibilities included staff matters, budgetary management, and all matters of day-to-day operations as well as the design and maintenance of the learning model central to the work and success of the College. Planning, College developments, publicity and fund-raising as well as participation in Dartington's other projects were all aspects of the role. A small team with the skills to design, plan and publicise an ever-changing programme of courses and facilitate the needs of a range of students, assisted the Director.

It was always clear to me that it was the Trustees who 'paid the piper' and it was they who therefore called the tune. In our case the 'tune' was to run a place where courses exploring the new ecological and spiritual worldview were held. The student, staff or helper groups could not turn it into anything else.

For example, each summer the College was closed so that the Dartington International Summer School of Music,[22] which is central to the overall vision of Dartington, could use the accommodation as part of their estate-wide five-week festival. This had been a decision taken as the College was opened, and was truly in the spirit of a trust thinking holistically about its activities. For the staff across the estate who had to bring about the transformation, it was an annual marathon: for students living in the College and completing their dissertations, it was an imposition: for those marketing the College, it was a wasted opportunity for running lucrative summer courses to help secure the College's perilous finances. On the other hand, it was a time when maintenance work in the main house could sometimes be fitted in, and a time when staff holidays could be taken. In short, this was an annual illustration of the fact that critical decisions about how the College could run were clearly within the ambit of the Trustees, who had responsibilities for more than the College. It was a particular expression of how the College and the Trust could be at odds within and between themselves.

Supporting the learning process

It was always the intention that there should be consistency between the curriculum and the teaching methods. Firstly, the emphasis was on people learning rather than being taught, and the College and its processes were designed to promote this. The processes were in themselves intended to be educative: process as education. Nonetheless, there was quite a lot of conventional teaching at the College. For people who were finding it more difficult to learn than they had hoped, I often found myself pointing out that in the same way that individuals had preferred styles of learning, teachers had their preferred styles of teaching. The most effective style of learning was therefore one which could tolerate even the most uncongenial teaching style. Individuals had to learn how to learn. Easier said than achieved!

At the root of the College's design principles was the intention to optimise learning opportunities and to create a transformative learning environment. 'Transformative' is a word used to describe a learning environment which encourages such a significant change in the students that the society of which they are part may also change. The College aimed not only to develop the individual students but to encourage change towards a fairer society and a better world. In Fritjof Capra's [23] Introduction to this book he also recognises this aspect of the College's function.

In a review of the College that Stephen Sterling [24] carried out in 2002, he said that:

> Schumacher College has been – and is still – a bold experiment that has achieved successful innovation both in developing and teaching ecological thought in a way that is extremely unusual, and in evolving a learning environment that works synergetically with the curriculum. Indeed, the College is distinct because its environment and operation are 'curriculum as lived experience', rather than a backdrop to formal instruction.

One of the key reasons why the College operations are "curriculum as lived experience" is the presence of a facilitator on each course.

Facilitation

Following the detailed review in 1993 of the College's work and its subsequent restructuring, it was decided to appoint a facilitator for each course to ensure that each individual participant could learn most effectively. This was (and has remained) a crucial role, especially as the work of the College became more complex and there was less staff capacity to carry out this function. There are several purposes to be fulfilled.

The facilitator links the course group into the College systems, which may be confusing and seem impersonal or routine. A person who is familiar with our ways can explain how things work and why they are as they are. Being able to work with differences in the various learning styles of course participants, facilitators can also prepare students for the contrasts between the teaching styles of the various visiting teachers. If they have sufficient skill, they can help the teacher deliver creative learning opportunities such as using the arts and crafts activities to help people begin to embody their learning. In particular, they can stimulate reflection and review of the processes of the course and the wider College and the learning that is taking place. Where this happens there can be feedback to the Director about the progress of the course so that action can be taken to address any issues if necessary.

We did not have sufficient funds to pay a facilitator, and in recompense for their contribution they were given a free place in the course they were facilitating. Another reason for avoiding engaging a permanent facilitator was to retain a diversity and freshness of style of facilitation. Instinctively we felt that long-term facilitation would be so demanding that no one individual could sustain this role over an extended period, yet it was clear that it was vital to have such a role if course participants were to learn most effectively. At the same time, having a facilitator to take care of students' learning needs enabled the regular staff to focus on the demands of their routine tasks. Usually, people who had attended previous courses at the College carried out the role because they would know the environment, and we at the College would have a fair idea of whether they would be able to manage what we saw as a critically important task. Often the individuals who carried out this role were highly experienced and skilled.

Paul Roberts,[25] who with three others devoted considerable time and expertise in supporting the 1993 review of the College, wrote to me recently about the "mysterious, magical and profound" experience he and others had at the College. He went on to say that it seemed to him to be a "fundamental dilemma about the need to create this experience afresh for each course group, and the high demands and even burdens this imposed on the people working at the College, which itself had the need of any organisation to have its routines, its established ways of doing things. Also, I felt the more I personally was involved at the College, and the more I could see how the 'magic' was created, and the work that was necessary behind the scenes to create the magic (like seeing how the conjuror does his tricks), the harder it was for me to appreciate the magic, though I continually observed its workings on other people." The group of whom Paul was one helped those of us permanently at the College, who were expected to create this profound learning experience for everyone who came to the College, to resolve that the role of facilitator was critical – not only to the success of each course but to the sanity of the permanent staff!

The role created is a demanding one. A facilitator might be approached by a participant for help at any time of the day. The question of how available they were willing to be, was handled differently by each facilitator. In deciding how to help the students the facilitators needed to learn when it made sense to show the students how to satisfy their own needs and when to do things for them. They needed to be able to support the students and, sometimes, to challenge them or the course leaders themselves about how the learning process was proceeding. They had to curb their own ambitions for personal learning in the interests of serving the needs of the group. To do this work selflessly was truly a service to the College and to the students, but it took its toll on those who took up the challenge of doing it well.

Paul Roberts thought "we did it well, with a light touch which did not get in the way of the unfolding experience of being at Schumacher College". He says he saw facilitation primarily as a safety net, to be used if there were particular difficulties or problems with any course. The facilitator is also the person who managed some aspects of the reflection and review of the course, though there are other opportunities for regular reflection built into daily routines. As well as having the facilitator to smooth the learning process, there are certain practices during courses which are designed for the same purpose.

Regular routines to facilitate learning

It is easy to forget that participants can be overwhelmed when they arrive at the College. For some this could be their first time in England and, too, the first time to employ an unfamiliar language. Sometimes they might find it easier to understand non-native English speakers, and occasionally they find some accents totally unintelligible.

We have to be careful to introduce students to each other, students to staff, visitors to the residents, and residents to guests several times in order that everyone feels comfortable with the other people in the College.

Hence, on the first evening of each course there is a welcoming meeting where people introduce themselves, however they wish, and the new residents begin to get to know each other. To help ensure that everyone knows what everyone else at the College is doing, we introduce anyone who visits the College, usually at the Morning Meetings. It also became clear that some of the local visitors who regularly attend the Open Evenings (when the College welcomes the local community) want the student group introduced to them. Most students are willing to go through this ritual again, if only briefly, especially since they realise some more new friends might result.

The first introductory circle for each new course is held in the library, and I always tried to establish an atmosphere of quietness, calm and respect so that people will feel welcomed, accepted and free to be their best. We always encourage everyone living at the College to come and introduce themselves and meet the new group at this meeting. From the perspective of the staff, it is here that it is possible to anticipate the difficulties participants might experience if, for example, someone is hard of hearing or has language problems. For new participants, this first meeting is intended to communicate a warm welcome and make them feel secure and 'at home' by anticipating some of their concerns. People living at the College but unable to be present at the meeting are also introduced. Safety regulations about fire and security are explained; people are told how they can contact their homes, and where they will find a hot-water bottle. They are invited to spend some time together socially in the bar so that ideally, before going to bed, they feel safe, secure and welcome. As their stay lengthens, we take care in new situations to introduce people time after time in order to make them feel valued and involved in the life of the College.

To mirror the beginning of a new programme there is always a closing circle. Many people find the process of saying goodbye difficult to handle, and this ritual helps. The circle is almost always held in the library, and attended by as many staff and helpers as can come, as well as the departing course members. Again we sit in a circle and start from stillness. People are invited to say anything they wish, but are discouraged from engaging in a conversation. If no-one has anything to say, there is a meditative and companionable silence. The ritual creates an opportunity where people can say their farewells formally and end their time at the College on a quiet rather than a frantic note. At the same time I always welcome the group into the larger Schumacher family made up of previous course participants. I encourage them to keep in touch with us and with each other for support after they return home. This practice eases the leaving process for many who might otherwise find it very difficult.

Reflection and review

Built into the daily routines are regular periods of reflection. As well as the scheduled times for meditation or the times each individual takes for him- or herself, each Friday afternoon the facilitator conducts a group review of the processes, the successes and the difficulties of the previous week. First of all this helps the facilitator work with the course participants if they need to do more to grasp the meaning of the previous week's classes. It also enables the facilitator to gather sufficient material to feed back to the College Director, and to pass on to new teachers arriving over the weekend. From the students' perspective, it helps individuals begin to consolidate their learning and to prepare for new teachers.

The other space where students can discuss their progress formally but confidentially, with a member of staff and in a small group, is once a week after the morning meeting. Each day one of the five small groups meets for this purpose. It is up to the member of staff and the members of the group as to whether concerns expressed at this meeting go any further. It is not intended to cover ground about the course content, but to reflect on what each individual is getting from the course and to consider how working together in the small group promotes their learning. Away from the larger group, individuals can explore here how they are learning, what their difficulties are, and in the final analysis raise issues confidentially where they are not happy about something. With skilled support, issues about personal learning difficulties can be resolved, complaints about the learning process, teachers or facilitators can be raised for staff to follow up, and a mutual support group be created enabling members to stay in touch after the course ends.

Meditation

The particular place for reflection that was programmed into the daily timetable was meditation. Each day at 7.15 a.m. (and in some courses at 6 p.m.) some of the students and staff would make their way to the room set aside in the main building for half an hour's silent meditation. Once a week Satish leads a guided meditation focusing on breathing, but otherwise it is a silent period. The person who has led the great majority of the sessions over the years is William Thomas,[26] who lived in one of the student rooms in the residential accommodation. I asked him how he would describe the role of meditation at the College. This was his response.

"The morning meditation sessions at Schumacher have always been optional and non-denominational. How, then, can they be of much value when attendance dwindles to four or five diehards in the second and third weeks of a course? Reflection in many forms was built into the curriculum at the College from the start. Classroom discussion, small group dialogue, companionship in essential work, Gaian exercises on Dartmoor and Goethean analysis of growing things, are the kinds of ingredients we like at Schumacher. It doesn't matter if some people find these things too New Age and wander off on their own – the important thing is the presence of the opportunity. It is like the presence of the wilderness – most of us don't go there much, but it is good to know it's there and we could go if we wanted to.

"Everyone has their own take on meditation – some see it as spiritual, others as therapy, others as deliberate mind management. Necessarily and appropriately, the usual introduction to meditation at the College comes from Satish Kumar, one of the founders. I once heard him sum up his message in a single sentence, and it echoed Aldous Huxley's final advice. 'We know when it is that we are happy: we are happy when we are kind.' The half-hour of meditation at Schumacher College is kindness to the day."

David Cadman writes of the meditation, "I remember some especially deep moments of silence. In a world devoted to pace and entertainment it is perhaps extraordinary that it should be so."

Setting the tone each day

Not everyone chooses to go to morning meditation, but everyone is encouraged to go to the meeting of the whole community held each morning at 8.30 in the main hall. There is always a reading, usually chosen by one of the course participants. At this meeting guests are introduced and announcements about significant events for the day are made. Not only does this remind people what will happen in their own course, but it means that everyone can keep abreast of how other students or visitors are spending their day. One of the most valued aspects of the College is making unexpected connections, and it is by keeping people informed in this way that such connections are promoted.

The small work groups

After morning meeting the student group and some of the staff disperse to carry out together certain communal work. Earlier I mentioned that it was always the intention that the College be self-sufficient in carrying out such tasks as preparation of the food, washing the dishes, cleaning the communal areas, preparing the spaces for the day's activities, and attending to the shared facilities in the residential accommodation. On some occasions there were also opportunities to work in the gardens. This is also the time when one of the work groups meets with a member of staff to reflect on their learning.

In carrying out the communal work, students quickly get to know the College and soon begin to feel at home within it. They are introduced to the practices we have adopted in cleaning and cooking. Often I would observe that in mindfully cleaning the lavatories they might reflect on the 'throw away', polluting and wasteful nature of our civilisation. For some who have never carried out domestic chores such work can be eye-opening, and they learn how rewarding it can be. Often, women who feel burdened by the need to feed their families, recapture the joy of working with others to create meals. It is an aspect of the curriculum which in prospect new students may find quite daunting, but in a couple of days it clearly becomes both acceptable and enjoyable.

In order to ensure that maximum diversity is created in each small work group, College staff design in advance membership of the five work groups. The aim is to have young and old, female and male, and as many different nationalities and backgrounds as possible. We also aim to split partners, or parents and their children, so each person has the best chance to be uninhibited by their own histories. The groups that are formed would be unlikely to have formed if the course members were left to themselves to do it. It is in such a context that members are challenged by the behaviour of fellow group members, and surprising learning can take place through engaging with those they would not necessarily have chosen as work-mates.

These small groups can acquire such importance by the end of the course that their members stay in touch for years after they have left the College. As David Cadman has said, "Theirs is the friendship of those who have worked together in Love."

The rest of the day

After the work groups finish, there is a brief break before the morning classes begin at 10 a.m. They last until 1 p.m. when lunch, largely prepared by catering staff and helpers, is served. The classes are often an intensive and rigorous time, and usually provide sufficient intellectual

William Thomas

Julia Ponsonby

Inge Page

Brian Goodwin

Satish Kumar and Vandana Shiva

Wolfgang Sachs

Anne Phillips

Fritjof Capra and Satish Kumar

HRH the Prince of Wales during a visit to the College in 2006

Class with Marion Woodman

Performance after mask-making workshop

A morning kitchen work group

Waste sorting in the College scullery

'Living Machine' student project

Student doing community work

Stephan Harding teaching about Deep Ecology

James Hillman leading a seminar in the central hall

Field trip on Dartmoor with Stephan Harding

Morning exercise

Story telling at a soirée

input for the rest of the day. Teachers have a variety of styles, from the didactic to the participative: the former can elicit challenges, especially from those who have difficulty following, and the latter annoys those who want their learning to come on a plate.

The afternoons are deliberately programmed to unfold at a different pace from the mornings. Some may be spent on local field trips, when the students can be introduced by Stephan Harding to Gaia Theory and Deep Ecology, and to the beauty of the local countryside. Sometimes students may choose to remain free: others meet to take forward the investigations prompted by a shared interest.

Most evenings, before the evening meal, there is a time for one or two of the small groups to meet again with the Scholar-in-Residence to reflect on the course. At the same time one of the other small groups is preparing the supper, and yet others might be taking the opportunity to meditate.

After supper, participants are encouraged to make presentations to each other about their lives and work at home. It can be in these situations that significant relationships carrying forward beyond the course, are forged and cemented. On other evenings there may be guest speakers, or specially organised events such as the Friday evening soirée.

One of the regular evening routines of the College is to hold an Open Evening for the local community each Wednesday when there is a three-week course in progress. We want to develop a following of local people who are really interested in the work of the College. It is almost always very popular. As a mark of courtesy to the speaker and the guests, the meeting is usually hosted by a key member of staff. Biscuits made in the kitchen are offered with tea after the talk is over.

Balance

It may sound as if the College is a serious, demanding sort of place. It is, but there is always plenty of love, laughter and fun. Periods of intense experience, whether of hard physical work or demanding intellectual exploration, are balanced by contrasting activities. As an example, the friendships at the heart of the College are cemented at the soirées, held on both Friday nights and the last night of each course. These times are occa-sions for celebrations. Master of Ceremonies is usually our ubiquitous William Thomas (the person describing the meditation). Here he explains, as he usually does each Thursday at morning meeting:

"No matter how many times I tell groups that the soirée is not a singsong and not meant to be hard work, people do insist on bringing circle dances and lapsing into a communal 'Summertime, and the living is easy'. I really don't know what to do about it. On a Friday evening after a hard week you can't get heavy-handed with people, so off it goes, as usual, in an unanticipated direction. At Schumacher, this entertainment has always varied in quality, from the unskilled right down to the really terrible. When the standard is sufficiently low there is no need for self-consciousness, and quite surprising offerings regularly appear. We gather in an untidy circle by candlelight at about nine o'clock in the central hall, after the bar has already been open for about half an hour. It is Friday, and the course members have by then got to know each other and the resident community quite well. In that same room at our 8:30 morning meeting, I have tried to explain: 'It is an alternative to the monolithic entertainment we have become used to, where we all stare in the same direction at one thing. The idea is that each person brings an offering which they have given thought to earlier, not a spontaneous bursting into the songs of Lennon and McCartney. The ingredient of thought is what makes each offering precious: a different glimpse into a life, and a droplet of something personal. It does not have to be amusing, and it does not have to be good.'

"On one of the very rare occasions of a security breach at Schumacher, a couple of youths were prowling the cars in the front car park, trying the door-handles. By a startling coincidence that Friday evening, the group of mainly male participants on the 'Sustainability in Business' course had gone out into the garden for a group photo in their costumes. They closed in on the two youths more out of curiosity than outrage. These two looked up and took in for several speechless moments the spectacle confronting them: eight or ten quite big men, all in women's clothing and make-up, staring at them like visitors from another planet. But back to the soirées: the main thing is the ability to endure the embarrassing silences between offerings. It is in those silences that the secret of life comes nearly within our grasp: the world, ultimately, is poor quality entertainment – but the personal element makes it infinitely precious. And then someone who has said nothing all week gets up and astonishes us all."

Learning resources at Schumacher College

To support the learning there are two key resources at the College that have been built up over the years: the library and the craft room. The library is the one which has absorbed the most energy, expertise and money to develop. Its unique character was acknowledged when the

University of Plymouth was assessing Schumacher for its suitability to run Masters level courses (see Chapter 8), and the library won much positive comment.

The library

The Schumacher library represents perhaps the most concentrated collection of books on the ecological and spiritual worldview anywhere. It isn't necessarily that the books it holds are obscure or difficult to find in other libraries (although many of them are). It's more that, at Schumacher, all these books exist side by side in one space. Anyone could spend a few hours perusing the shelves and get a pretty good feeling for the scope and ambition of an holistic education and the ecological and spiritual worldview.

The library now contains about 6,000 key texts by scholars-in-residence and other authors on the new paradigm, and reflects its deep intellectual and cultural roots. The MSc in Holistic Science programme influenced the library's evolution because it shifted the College's intellectual centre of gravity towards scientific enquiry. For the course's first few years many books were acquired on Goethean Science, Gaia, Chaos, Complexity and related topics.

The way the library had originally been set up was idiosyncratic, but it is small enough for one person to come to know what is there. As the years have passed, the library has become more intensively used and has become an increasing draw to students and to potential helpers who offer the College their services so they can have free access to it over an extended period for their own personal study projects.

Craft room

Before the College even opened its doors, the planning group decided to offer all students the opportunity to work one afternoon each week with a skilled craftsperson. The decision reflected our sense that craft skills were in themselves of value, and not simply an antidote to a predominantly intellectual and cerebral education. Nearby the College was Dartington's Craft Education Centre, where three outstanding craftspeople worked. One was a wood worker, carving and turning in his workshop. Next door a bookbinder and letterpress printer had her workshop. Her neighbour was a painter and print-maker. All three were interested in the ecological work of the College, and were enthusiastic that with four afternoons spread across the five-week course they could help the course participants acquire some useful craft skills.

This decision was consistent with an educational philosophy which valued an holistic approach to learning and aspired to bring together the sciences and the arts. It recognised the place of crafts not only in their own right, but in the development of hand skills and in offering an alternative way to explore and come to understand the world. It was not the intention that course participants went home as accomplished printers, for example – though some did start on new paths – but that by participating in this activity they were able to experience in an entirely new way their overall learning from the course.

It was with some reluctance then, that this aspect of the course structure was eliminated when the length of the courses was reduced from five to three weeks. There would not be enough time within the shorter programme to sustain an introduction to a craft skill at the same time as following all the other important aspects of the College's curriculum. Thus a substitute had to be found where in-house craft resources could be developed to serve a similar educational purpose.

A room at the Old Postern was allocated for craft materials, and one of the staff, Julia Ponsonby, introduced the resources and initially ran workshops on mask-making. These were intended to enable students, through working with their hands, to begin to explore the concepts that were raised in the intellectual part of the programme, to 'em-body' their learning. One group, who were studying globalisation, through their masks created a cast of characters from a community in the global south. There was the beautiful Indian woman with bleached and straightened hair who wore contact lenses to make her eyes look blue; there was the wicked capitalist, be-suited and chewing a cigar; there was the ox from the village and a new tractor; the tourist whose eyes were represented by a camera, and so on. When it came to the Friday night soirée, the masks were donned and the play was performed. One of the course members took the idea home to work with fellow villagers in raising awareness of what was happening in their community.

Still on every programme there are always a few people for whom the craft room plays a vital part in their grappling with the intellectual work. Often it simply enables them to do something completely absorbing so they might unconsciously reflect on their experiences. For others, it creates a chance to work with their fellows in a different context and experience new insights. It is the kind of congenial atmosphere that relaxes almost everyone and frees the mind and body, allowing learning to take place.

Focal points

- After a couple of years the unsustainable finances of the College triggered a root-and-branch review. It was recognised that the College had gained confidence and expertise in its new work, yet there were changes which could be made building on the hard-won experience of running courses for two years. For example, each new course did not need to be redesigned from first principles. There were essential ingredients which had been recognised in all the most successful courses which could in future be planned into all courses.
- Whatever the particular situation, a new project needs such a review in order to see if it is true to its original intentions, and whether there are changes which might be introduced to strengthen or improve it in any way. To what extent is the project realising the dream?
- Some changes strengthen the project by standardisation or simplification: others may introduce new levels of complexity.

Chapter 8

Programme development

BUGS IN A BOWL

Han Shan, that wonder filled Chinese poet of a thousand years ago, said
We're just like bugs in a bowl, All day going around never leaving their bowl.
I say, That's right! Every day climbing up
The steep sides, sliding back
Over and over again, Around and around
Up and back down.
Sit in the bottom of the bowl, head in your hands,
Cry, moan feel sorry for yourself.
Or look around. See your fellow bugs.
Walk around.
Say, Hey, how you doin'?
Say, Nice bowl!

– Introduced to the College by Zen priest and chef Ed Brown, author of *Tomato Blessings and Radish Teachings*

Throughout the history of the College modifications have been made to the curriculum. It has never been intended to run the same courses time and again: rather the intention was to revisit key themes from different perspectives. Declining recruitment to College courses after the first years suggested that programming policy might need re-examination. Courses were shortened, and some aspects of the early short courses were eliminated. In sharpening its focus, the College eventually identified particular groups of students, such as the business people and teachers, and programmes were developed to meet their particular needs.

The Masters in Holistic Science

In the review begun in 1993 it was questioned whether students might like to get credits for their study, and there began a process of gaining accreditation from the University of Plymouth, the local university. The Masters Credits Scheme created a sound working relationship with key people at the University. Under the scheme, any student attending a designated short course could submit a piece of work that they had done during the course, for consideration for Masters Level Credits. At that time methods of assessment were becoming more flexible and imaginative. Indeed, students were now able to negotiate their own study and method of assessment, so it was possible for an individual to study for credits without involving the rest of the group. Those choosing this option needed to set the focus for their study from the start, so their freedom, both intellectually and socially, was more constrained. At the College, Stephan Harding administered the scheme and acted as Tutor to those taking Credits. It was this work that prepared the ground in which a new full-time Masters course could be proposed.

The reasons for trying to set up a Masters level course of study were several. Moves towards it probably began in 1995. Since the mainstream paradigm is built on a scientific perspective, it was decided that any challenge to it from the College would need to be based on some serious and sustained scientific study at an advanced level. There was also the pragmatic decision to try to fill all available bedrooms, in order to generate the maximum income. Somewhere in between these two extremes there was the sense that a College with a small permanent body of full-time students would be a more attractive place to study. It was the view that whilst the short course participants would benefit from an atmosphere of continuing rigorous enquiry in the College, the experience of a Masters student group would be enhanced by the passage through the College of visiting teachers and students.

One of the first decisions I had made when I took over as Director of the College in 1993 was that the maximum number of participants on short courses should be twenty-five. This was based on my view of what was the optimal size of an effective learning group, and was balanced against the financial considerations of not recruiting the largest group we could accommodate. In practice this meant that even when a course was fully subscribed, there were always some College bedrooms left empty. All these spare spaces were concentrated in the smallest residential accommodation building and, for reasons of economy, we simply closed down that building. Whilst this enabled us to minimise expenses, it meant we were not maximising our income. On the other hand it meant that there was the space for another compatible activity if one were to appear.

After the educational success of the initial short courses, and after we had established a relationship with Plymouth University to accredit them, we began to plan setting up a longer and deeper course of study in the area of the new sciences. If we wanted to comment with more authority on the current scientific worldview, we needed to be investigating alternatives to the current paradigm.

We might equally have set up a programme in economics for similar reasons. Yet an offer was made to the developmental biologist Professor Brian Goodwin to help the College develop a Masters course and he jumped at the offer, seeing it as a great opportunity and honour.

Prior to coming to the College, Brian Goodwin had been developing a course with Margaret Colquhoun[27] on the New (Post-Modern) Science. It was this course that provided the basis of the proposal that was eventually put to the University of Plymouth. Its main components were Chaos, Complexity, and Gaia, with an experiential part based on Goethean Science. Everyone had anticipated resistance from the University to this proposal, so we were delighted to find instead that we were knocking on an open door. This was largely because over the previous years the Credits scheme had established a sound working relationship with key people at the University. Within the University's academic and administrative hierarchy, this programme had established our credibility as an institute of advanced learning having both the teaching and administrative resources to service the needs of the students.

Informal approaches to the University were not rebuffed, but the College had no funds to finance the development. Fortuitously Satish Kumar found a very generous benefactor who gave the College £120,000, which contributed to the development costs over three years. The submission turned out to be less difficult than anticipated for several reasons. The proposed leader of the programme, Brian Goodwin, was an internationally recognised scientist. Not only did the Plymouth University link person suggest the succinct and acceptable title of Holistic Science, but our work on the short course credits had been well received. In short, the groundwork we had put into our first links with the University paid off when we asked for approval of the rather unusual programme that had been devised.

Recently I contacted Professor Peter O'Neill[28] to ask him about his memories of the setting-up of the MSc. Like us all, his memory of the details has faded but his reply told us what it was that really swung the University towards validating our proposal. I quote his reply at length because it illustrates the potential that this mainstream academic institution saw in the 'idiosyncratic' college that was Schumacher, and why they were prepared to risk their own reputation in approving the MSc proposal. It provides pointers to the qualities and capacities, ranging from rigorous administrative systems to imaginative teaching approaches, that are required in a place such as Schumacher College if collaborations with the mainstream are sought. He wrote:

"I do not remember who first contacted me about the possibility of Plymouth validating an MSc at Schumacher. Though I was aware of the College, I did not have much idea of what courses were run. I talked to a number of people at Plymouth about the background of the College. It quickly became clear that Schumacher College had a good national and international reputation with regard to the quality of some of the speakers. However, it was also clear that the approach was not necessarily conventional and mainstream in terms of environmental content.

"I was not particularly in favour of the link, but was interested to meet the staff at Schumacher to see if 'we could do business'. I must say that I was very impressed with the realistic (to my mind) approach that you were supporting. I tended to work on the basis that if you have the right people carrying out a task, then there should be little need to interfere. Once the parameters are set, able people will more often than not produce good results. It seemed to me that the staff had worked out an approach to delivering an MSc standard course that would work in the context of Schumacher College. It was then a question of how we ensured that you successfully 'jumped' the validation hurdles. This was necessary to ensure credibility for your course and also, I guess, to provide protection for our good name. Again, the way the team buckled down to producing course documents that complied with our regulations, confirmed to me that we were not 'taking a risk' (as our Vice-Chancellor had suggested to me).

"The ethos at Schumacher was very different from that at a large University like Plymouth, where the extensive infrastructure means that basic costs are high and there is an almost industrial approach to higher education. The continuation of small, dare I say idiosyncratic, institutions is important, because they can experiment with new ideas and try new methods. In larger institutions there is a lot of internal competition that leads to people staying with the herd and being afraid of trying something until someone else has shown it works. Once I was convinced of your abilities I was very keen to help to clear a path for you to have your MSc up and running."

Thus the proposal was duly approved, and in April 1998 applications were invited from students for the year-long programme. For this first, experimental year, two applications were accepted, one from a Japanese business consultant and the other from a South African dentist. Such a group size was sustainable neither financially nor educationally, not being sufficiently diverse or challenging a learning group. In subsequent years, numbers increased until the optimum of thirteen students was reached. The dreams of a fuller and stronger College were fulfilled, and the efforts of the teachers to develop this new mode of enquiry were recognised (in conventional terms) in increasing numbers of outstanding examination results. Plymouth University's risk was rewarded with exceptional success. How some of these students have applied their learning is shown in Chapter 9.

Courses for business people and for teachers

Despite the interest in the year-long Masters programme, there remained a concern that most people could not find three weeks to attend one of the College courses let alone a whole year. It was therefore decided to offer one-week courses (Sunday to Friday) first of all for business people. We had been funded by the Tedworth Charitable Trust, which is one of the Sainsbury Trusts, to explore whether it was possible to offer the so-called Schumacher Experience to business people with the aim of bringing about profound changes in the way business is done. There was some question about whether business people would even spare a whole week, but at once courses filled and some key senior level staff attended.

Some feared that the outward appearance of the College and its community work would deter people from the mainstream business sector. Certainly, we never had a chance of attracting what I used to call 'the gold tap brigade'. Instead of en-suites, champagne and a servant class, the College offered an opportunity for business people to prepare each other's food and clean each other's lavatories. In the event, those who came here loved it. They buckled down to their community work and learning about sustainability with a vigour unrivalled by even the keenest MSc students. College staff were delighted to have them here, not least because they left it cleaner than when they arrived and did the work with such good grace. Some of the people who used their experience from the College most successfully were people who came on the Business and Sustainability courses. On one of the early programmes was the Managing Director of a massive UK civil engineering company, Peter Head. He now works for Arup directing a newly integrated business in urban design and development. American colleagues had recommended he take the opportunity to meet one of our teachers, Amory Lovins. He said Amory's stories "made me look down the other end of the telescope" and that he left the course with "a sense that there is an infinite opportunity for change and improvement that can be turned into commercial success in every sphere". He says that Schumacher College changed his life "because it developed me as a person and my knowledge at the same time".

The business course model was modified for teachers, and again some key individuals attended what we called the Roots of Learning courses. After the first flush of enthusiastic individuals it became increasingly difficult to recruit, despite the fact that these courses had been offered at a heavily subsidised rate in order to support teachers' attendance. The question of whether the College's marketing was sufficient to its increasingly complex task became obvious as the College diversified. On the other hand, it could have been that the courses were too long or took place in school holidays; that there were other courses competing to teach sustainability; or that the model of holistic education was simply too advanced for the average school labouring under the demands of the National Curriculum.

Focal points

- Having designed and established a learning model and confidence in its efficacy, the time came to deliberately target key groups who would benefit from the College's focus and multiply the impact of its work. Such expansion served the College's agenda. It targeted influential individuals who had the energy and resources to implement new ideas in the world of business, and teachers who could improve the learning environment in their own schools. In the case of the Masters course it provided a way to validate and work through some of the assumptions of the ecological and spiritual paradigm underpinning all the College's work.
- Through broadening, deepening and consolidating a project its integrity is continually tested and its impact multiplied.

Chapter 9

From study to action

"Schumacher College was a rare week in my life: a chance to be where people are trying to live in the ways they'd like the planet to live. I don't just mean the incredible vegetarian cooking, or the communal work; I mean the intense but gentle learning, the respectful but challenging dialogue, the deep but practical thinking, all amidst a countryside so beautiful it's hard to describe. My whole family was sad to go home, and eager to return."

– Bill McKibben, author of *The End of Nature* and Scholar-in-Residence 1999

"May all your trails be crooked, winding, lonesome, dangerous, leading to the most amazing view…where something strange and more beautiful and more full of wonder than your deepest dreams waits for you."

– Edward Abbey, *Desert Solitaire*

One way of assessing the success of the College is to look at what former students tell us have been the outcomes for them. Broadly, there are four different ways of being a student at the College.

- First there are short courses, which initially were five weeks but have since become three weeks or less.
- Since the MSc was introduced, students in this group have largely been based at the College for the best part of a year.
- The third category included those brought as part of a group by other institutions, usually for a week, to experience the College's processes and focus on ecology.
- The fourth group are those who have attended a course and return to act as volunteer/helpers at the College. During their time here they often pursue their own studies which lead them to establish projects on their return home.

Even though the courses at Schumacher College have varied significantly in length, past participants, regardless of which courses they attended, seem to say broadly similar things about its effect on them. Some claim to have been transformed by their time at the College. This chapter gives just a few representative examples of what individuals have told us they have done as a result of having been here.

Short Course students

I have categorised the outcomes of attendance in four broad categories: campaigning and activism; starting community projects; changes in their own ways of living; and changes in their own attitudes.

Campaigning and activism

- I used the course as a personal springboard into campaigning against genetic engineering.
- The learning contributed to the creation of my book. (e.g. *The Ecology of Health* by Robin Stott)
- Building on earlier work for my PhD, I established a Charter of Human Responsibility in New Zealand.
- Several ex-students based around the globe told us they are working on setting up something similar to Schumacher College.
- One of our alumni has become deeply involved in Shipping and Emissions Trading and more widely in green politics.
- Many have become more active in their local areas and are contributing to policy making.
- One has become a Member of the London Sustainability Commission.
- One has spent many years developing energy-efficient hydrogen transport and has been exploring methods of getting it accepted in the mainstream car manufacturing industry.

Community projects

- Several have set up food co-operatives in their own city or community.
- Many have established study or action groups using skills and knowledge acquired at the College. For example, one participant from a religious community in Australia set up a study group which resulted in the publication of a regular ecological and spiritual magazine.

- One has designed and set up a new educational ecovillage.
- A participant from the Philippines has set up with colleagues a Centre of Environmental Ethics at her University there.
- Some have returned home to work with others to found networks such as community-supported agriculture schemes (CSAs).
- Many have promoted sustainable community development in their locality.

Changes in ways of living

- Many begin a formal or informal course of study focusing on their own eco-development.
- Some left their previous job to start something new they felt 'made sense'.
- Some saw their whole work and life's direction change.
- Many rebuild their own homes and gardens applying the ecological principles they learned here.

Attitudinal changes

- They made new friends whose values they shared.
- They remain in contact with others from their course group for many years.
- They leave feeling enriched, widened, and able to structure their future reading and study.
- They gain inspiration from the College itself and individuals of high quality who teach there.
- Many develop a sense of responsibility, almost of duty or obligation, to put into the world what they have learnt.

MSc students

MSc students generally stay at the College for a whole year. During their first term they are introduced to the basic principles of Holistic Science. They work intensively with two key teachers (Brian Goodwin and Stephan Harding), some visiting teachers, and each other. Alongside this they are living intensively in a fairly small community and as each new course group arrives, they meet waves of people of all ages and many experiences, from all over the world.

In the second term they begin work on their own chosen area of study, and work individually on their dissertations. By then they have developed a strongly supportive network within the course group, and are able to help each other through any difficulties that emerge. Often, having chosen interdisciplinary topics for their dissertations, they work together to complete their projects.

Within this context their personal worldviews are challenged and tested. They develop strong notions about how they want to spend the rest of their lives to make a difference in the world. For many, a community orientation continues in their work. Several create their own jobs, thus enabling them to work holistically in their chosen field. I have divided MSc student feedback into three areas: many created their own opportunities to enable them to facilitate the work they now wanted to do; they made invaluable connections and developed new marketable skills; and were personally transformed.

Creation of new opportunities

Some students founded new organisations or projects, sometimes with others, to enable them to follow their life's dream. Several aspire to create a place of learning like Schumacher College.

- One works as a consultant in California with 'big business' on sustainability promoting zero waste, carbon neutrality, renewal energy use.
- Another is working in Europe in the same field of business consultancy.
- In Ecuador, one is a consultant involving the local community in the work, and with them designing and building composting lavatories for tourists.
- One has undertaken environmental consultancy in Antarctica and has been conducting research on a penguin colony.
- The same person is a television presenter in Chile focusing on environmental issues.
- One is working to protect ancient trees in Alaska as a public lands conservationist.
- One is planting medicinal trees for health, in south Devon, England, working with volunteers and local schools.
- A South African student has set up a scheme assessing conservation projects there and linking them to corporate donors in South Africa.
- Alongside his main employment, one has established an NGO with the

mission of incubating small for-profit micro-manufacturing enterprises in developing countries to develop and sell in local markets a portfolio of open-source renewable and intermediate technologies such as wind turbines, solar systems etc.

Several students have built on their holistic studies at Schumacher College and gone on to do a PhD focusing on aspects of community transformation / societal change. One works in north-east Wyoming in the tribal homelands of the Shoshone and Northern Arapaho tribes, looking at the cultural and ecological links in lands designated as some of the Earth's most cherished wildlands.

Developed marketable skills and made contacts
- All students note that they developed a range of marketable skills, for example, more advanced computer modelling and other practical skills such as diverse modes of enquiry.
- They say they learnt to focus on quality rather than quantity in their work.
- Everyone established links with former teachers. For some this led to teaching and research opportunities.

Personal transformation
- Specifically, students say that they have made life-long relationships.
- They developed a deep connection to Gaia and Earth as a living being.
- Some have gone on to try to change cultural attitudes in their own society.
- Many found a philosophical foundation and a coherent framework for their subsequent work.
- For many it was a period of deep joy.

External groups

Some individuals are brought to the College by other institutes with whom they are studying. The most established example of this is the Masters in Responsibility in Business, taught by The University of Bath. It is offered as a distance learning programme, interspersed with week-long courses of intense group study at a variety of venues. Often the first of these intensives for each group is held at Schumacher College, where they are introduced to an ecological worldview. These groups bring their own staff, but follow the College's learning models. Schumacher College's own staff introduce ecological thinking and take the students on field trips into the remote parts of our environment up on Dartmoor.

One of their teachers writes that "learning about deep ecology and Gaia theory offers a profound challenge to programme participants. For many, it changes their sense of who they are as humans in relation to the Earth, and this penetrates and deeply challenges their practice as organisational members."

Paul Dickinson is one of their students who had a remarkable experience at Schumacher College. He writes as follows about how he was affected and what he did about it.

> "As a result of the visit to the College, I dedicated my life to working against climate change, because of the impact of the College and in particular the ecologist Stephan Harding. We were walking in the woods and he spoke of climate change. The clarity and certainty that Stephan used to communicate with me was striking. I now know that the Gulf Stream delivers to the UK the heat equivalent to that from millions of power stations, and that it might indeed cease to operate. It has done so before. Above all what Stephan did was to grow in me the fear that there would be a profound change in the continuity of the world from that of my happy childhood to an uncertain and quite possibly unpleasant future.

> "It inspired me to set up the Carbon Disclosure Project (CDP) which now employs 10 people directly and as many again in partner organisations. We have permanent offices and partners in London, New York, Tokyo, Paris and Stockholm and we work closely with partner organisations across the world. We represent 300 institutional investors with assets of some $40 trillion and on their behalf we require 2000 of the world's largest corporations to disclose information about their greenhouse gas emissions."

Helpers

Having attended a course and having liked what they have seen, some people offer to return and give their service to help the College in its work. They often stay as helpers/volunteers for an extended period, and sometimes bring a project to make best use of the resources at the College during their time here. One such person was one of the College's first young students, Morag Gamble, from Australia. She first came in its second year, and says that whilst here she was able to "clarify my thinking and my values, and . . . my life's work became visible to me." She continues:

> "I left [the College] with an overwhelming sense of hope, positivity and clarity. I had met people from all around the world who were embracing the ecological paradigm and creating livelihoods, lifestyles and projects based on it. I had a sense that even though I was one person doing small local projects, I was part of a much larger movement of change globally – a positive change – and I felt honoured to be one of the catalysts for change in my local community. Since, I have always tried to link our local projects with others around the world."

In the following years she returned to attend more courses at the College as she developed the skills needed to set up several projects (all based in Australia) but working also in Asia-Pacific, the Americas and Europe. SEED International, which aims through ecodesign and ecoliteracy to bring about a sustainable future, is the umbrella covering much of her activity, and offers courses, facilitates community change and produces publications about sustainable ways of living. She and her husband co-founded Crystal Waters College in Queensland, Australia, which offers an holistic educational experience based on Schumacher College. It also designs programmes for communities wishing to set up ecovillages, and Morag has taught such groups in twenty countries. She has also set up a City Farm in Brisbane and helped establish the Australian City Farms and Community Gardens Network. In 2003 she returned to Schumacher College to teach a course on ecodesign.

As a helper, she had sufficient time at the College to develop and clarify a strong sense of direction for the rest of her life. Over the subsequent fifteen years she has gradually realised in her life the vision she glimpsed here as a twenty-three-year-old. She is an example of someone who has become an activist bringing into the world the ecological and spiritual change she first learned about at Schumacher College

Chapter 10

Paradoxes and challenges in running the College

To some extent the College was set up to illustrate the values of the new paradigm. At the same time, in many respects it was working within the old paradigm. There were therefore points at which the practices of the College disappointed some expectations. They varied from the mundane to rather more fundamental issues.

Students and teachers travelling from all over the world to Schumacher College

The carbon emissions from the travel of both students and teachers are part of the excessive consumption of fossil fuels that is leading to global warming. Our critics would prefer that the students were so local that the College did not contribute to this problem. In fact there seem to be good reasons why, as we move towards a post-oil economy and society, this traffic should continue. The international mix, sometimes from as many as twenty countries, including those from the global south, on a course of twenty-five students, enhances and deepens the quality of everyone's experience. Students return home with a fuller understanding of the critical issues of our time, seen from a wide perspective. Usually students stay here for several weeks or more for intensive study. They make a range of contacts who are able and willing to give them ongoing support via the internet when they initiate new projects in their local communities. Whilst there is an urgency to limit our consumption of fossil fuels, it is also important to promote affection and understanding between nations who will soon find themselves competing for limited resources.

Charging fees

The whole question of charging fees for the courses met much opposition, particularly from UK-based people. Many people, brought up in a society where much if not all of their education had been provided free of charge by the state, thought that 'education should be free'. Whilst we all would have liked to agree, the College had many expenses and received no subsidy for any of its work from the state. The College kept its costs to a minimum, and generated income and grants for bursary schemes where possible (though it was a challenge to avoid time and energy being diverted into ill-conceived income-generating schemes). Through staff efforts it was possible over the years to generate sufficient funds for more than a quarter of the students to receive some bursary support to attend the courses.

Nevertheless every year there were deficits, and it was The Dartington Hall Trust which shouldered them. Quite simply the College could not have survived without charging fees.

The balance of decision-making between The Dartington Hall Trust and the College

The Trustees had set the overall direction of the College and had delegated the management of the College to the Director. As in any organisation, the Director was expected to ensure that the Trust's objectives were served. Yet the College's staff and students expected that the College, as a new paradigm educational establishment, would behave according to values different from those they believed were held by the Trust. There was always the potential for differences to arise.

The extent of participation by both staff and students in making decisions was rather less than they would have wanted, and perhaps rather more than the Trust might have expected. It was sometimes said that decision-making was very slow, both within the College and in the wider Trust. Some, such as about expenditure, had to be reserved to the Trustees: a budget was set each financial year, and expenditure outside this was not possible. Other issues might be delegated to the whole or parts of the College community for resolution. The overall parameters had been set when the College was originally designed, yet there were certain limited areas where there could be discretion. These questions of authority, decision-making and responsibility exercised staff and students regularly, and there were those who resented the level of 'interference', as they saw it, by the Trust in the running of the College. The best example of this was each year when the International Summer School of Music took up residence in the College. A different kind of 'ownership' might have allowed different relations, but without the Trust the College would not have existed.

Experience of community

Many of those who came to the College, and indeed some of those who stayed for extended periods, believed that it was a community. In the sense that it consisted of a group of people with a shared intention, it was indeed so. However, it was not a self-determining community: it was a community with the shared intention of studying, but its members probably did not share the vision of exactly what it would be like. As a staff it was our job to create for each new group of students an experience of living in community. We had clarified this when we saw that some volunteers who had chosen to stay for extended periods began to manoeuvre the agenda around to the satisfaction of their own needs to live 'in community' rather than to serve the needs of a learning community.

To create the community experience was relatively straightforward whilst the courses were only three or even five weeks long. When, in parallel with the short courses, we began to run year-long courses for the MSc students, then the inherent difficulties of maintaining that we offered simply an 'experience of community' were exposed. Whilst the intellectual demands of the MSc students were satisfied by the regular arrival of new students and teachers, for those who had a need for a more settled community life, these changes presented a real challenge. One of the MSc teachers who lived in the College for several years said to me that it was in the MSc group that the shadow side of the way we ran the community revealed itself. Inevitably, with living for an extended period at the College, personal and interpersonal issues had more time to fully play themselves out.

Living with ambiguity and uncertainty

People sometimes feel slightly unnerved by the absence of lists of rules; they want an institution to spell out how it wants people to behave and how things should be done. The College is about learning, and to promote this I wanted us to avoid a rules-driven culture. In my experience most people carry out tasks in the best way that they know how, and I believe it is more creative to allow people to do this rather than demand conformity to a College norm. Everyone can learn when this freedom exists. Through this, as a simple example, I learned a very effective way of cooking artichokes from someone who lived in a part of California where artichokes were a primary crop: she knew how to prepare them in many different ways. From a different perspective, it's not possible to design enough rules to legislate against some of the things the students tried to do. For example, one of them began to wash carrots in hot water with washing-up liquid: no one would ever have thought to make a rule against that! It is better for staff to be alert to what is happening and to help students needing support, than to anticipate a problem and design learning opportunities out of the system.

This absence of detailed rules provides an opportunity for staff and students to learn to live with ambiguity and uncertainty. It leaves the field open for the emergence of co-responsibility; it is the ground upon which people can give of their best. If the overall context trusts to the individual's good will and if there are high expectations of everyone, then the absence of rules is the trigger for everyone's creativity to flower.

Changing our minds

Having made design decisions early in the College's life, sometimes circumstances arise which show us the early decision was not necessarily the right one, or possibly it was right only part of the time. There were going to be frequent occasions for reconsideration. Such circumstances applied to the College's relations with the wider educational establishment, with The Dartington Hall Trust and the Estate, and in our dealings with specific individuals, whether they were students or staff.

Early decisions were made because we believed them to be crucial to the creation of a 'new paradigm' College. To give just two examples; we decided not to become involved in the mainstream university accreditation system because of the pressure it put on the design of the learning. Secondly, it was our aim to develop a way of running the place which was congruent with the issues we were exploring. The first decision was effectively overturned when after three years we investigated the possibility of offering credits as a way of making the College more accessible to greater numbers of students. Entirely without our input, assessment methods had become more creative and it did not involve us in a huge compromise to seek accreditation for the courses from the local University. It would accredit the College because the job that we had undertaken was done well, and our way of doing things enhanced rather than diminished the standards students achieved. In practice these standards won us the University's respect for the academic rigour of our work. Thus it was that one of our earliest decisions was overturned, whilst another was reinforced.

Whilst the earliest intentions had been to keep ourselves out of the toils of the conventional educational system, and to influence it from outside, it seemed clear after those first short years that the mainstream had something to offer that would be to our advantage. This, of course, was accreditation of our courses at Masters Level. Also, as the years went on it was apparent that the University had benefited from its association with us. Its designation as a Centre of Excellence in the Teaching and Learning (CETL) of Education for Sustainability was partly attributed to the College's part in the proposal, and brought over £4 million to the University. Thus, on the ground, the issues of educating for sustainability in tertiary education were being introduced throughout the country partly through the work of the CETL and after all, that was what Schumacher College had been set up to achieve.

Relations with The Dartington Hall Trust and Estate

When Schumacher College opened on the Estate in 1991 some understood that this was the Trust's flagship educational activity: it was funded generously and located in one of the Trust's prime properties. Yet for most people on the Estate it probably seemed that really it was just an ordinary college run in a strange way. What most wouldn't have foreseen was that the students would begin to question the rest of the Trust's activities and the values that underpinned them.

For example, soon after the College was established there had been a decision to convert the estate land to organic production. Such a decision chimed well with the thrust of the College's work, and in some senses gave the College more credibility. It looked as if the Trust itself was embracing an ecological policy on its own land. The decision to reverse this move, taken just at the beginning of the new millennium and five years into the conversion programme, met with astonishment from College visitors unfamiliar with the ways of the Trust, and vocal opposition from the College and its students.

It highlighted the tension between the inevitable outcome of serious study of an ecological and spiritual vision for the twenty-first century, and the pragmatic management decisions taken by the Trust on behalf of its other activities. It illustrated the irreconcilable differences between the values of freewheeling activists and those responsible for the long-term security of the estate. Perhaps also it sowed doubt about the Trust's motivations among some key people at the College, and concern within the Trust about the reliability of the College. To some extent it marked the coming of age of the College and its striking out for an independent voice. If there had ever been a chance that land management decisions, or indeed any decisions on the Estate might be influenced by the College and the work that was being carried out there, then at this point that chance seemed lost – for how long remains to be seen.

It was a positive sign that in 2005 one of the Trust's key initiatives was to invite pioneering individuals who were experimenting with sustainable land use projects to become tenants on the Estate. This initiative was based on the work of one of the College's former MSc students, Julie Richardson. Elsewhere across the globe, former MSc students are busy implementing the new ideas they developed during their time at the College (see Chapter 9).

Protecting the learning environment for each group

As a result of its agenda to challenge received wisdom and the mainstream worldview, the College inevitably attracted as students those who questioned the way the College itself ordered its affairs. Sometimes such individuals questioned the policy of protecting the integrity of any particular learning group, on the basis that this was preventing freedom of access to the knowledge held by the course teacher.

By the practices adopted to manage the process for any group we intended to create a learning group which would gradually strengthen throughout the course and be available to sustain its members after the completion of the course. We took care to explain that the first lecture by a visiting teacher would be open to any member of the College community who might wish to attend, though the course group had priority for the teacher's attention. This was to create a focus for conversations between the different people in the College and to facilitate these exchanges. It was through such conversations that much learning took place. It was also to ensure that the MSc students had formal access to each visiting teacher if they so wished. We made it explicit that during the rest of the week the classes with the teacher would be reserved to the course group, except for the Open Evening. Sometimes this was challenged by some long-term students, helpers or even local residents, but the reason was that the creation and maintenance of the course group was taking priority over other considerations. Generally this principle was understood and accepted.

The reason this practice was adopted was that in our experience each individual has his or her own personality and learning needs, and these characteristics combined to create a unique identity for each group. Each individual has a particular relationship to the group as a whole and to its members, and for better or worse each group develops its own way of working. Therefore, in our view, the consistent membership of the group was important: if, for example, one of the members was sometimes not present or regularly late, most of the others would notice and (usually) be disturbed. Likewise, if, without explanation, prior knowledge or good reason, someone temporarily joined the group the others might well be upset. It was my sense that this was probably because of the level of commitment required to undertake one of the courses. Students not only had to find funds to pay fees and travel costs, but they had to give up a lot of time to be here. If someone joined the course without having made a similar commitment, and simply 'cherry-picked' lectures by a certain teacher, then students could be annoyed. This annoyance might extend towards anyone who simply dropped in. Because of these sensitivities, I felt it was important to respect the integrity of each group and to ensure their privacy was not violated.

When a particular guest wanted to join a group for some reason, my first instinct was to counsel against it. If there seemed to be a very good reason, I would try to ensure that the permission of the group was sought, and that the length of the visit was made clear. Often the person whose behaviour would threaten the privacy of the group would be the teacher who, with the best of intentions, might invite someone to join whom they thought could contribute to the group. To avoid this, it was important that the teacher knew about the College's policy. In order to reduce the possibility of this embarrassment it was also necessary that MSc students understood this policy. Many did, but for some, the appeal of special attention from a visiting teacher made them forget!

The practice of maintaining the integrity of the group took precedence over our instinct towards freedom and hospitality and our habit of avoiding rules. It was also probably the practice that was most often challenged.

Therapy

It had always been the intention that the College would be an educational rather than a therapeutic centre. We do not have the staff capable of handling some of the more serious personal crises that individuals might bring with them. Inclinations towards compassion for the suffering of our fellows might tempt us to try to help, but our expertise lay elsewhere. Whilst problems were by no means confined to American students, it was not uncommon, for example, for people from the USA to suddenly realise how American culture was feared and hated by many from the global south. Individual students sometimes felt they needed to assume personal responsibility for their nation's shortcomings. Others were distressed as their own vision of themselves as Americans was undermined. The College could usually support individuals through this level of difficulty, but did not have the resources to tackle deep psychological difficulties that individuals might bring with them. On such infrequent occasions we could only refer students elsewhere for psychological support. In order to avoid such situations we only had recourse to their application forms or in the case of bursary applicants or longer-term students, we had references.

Working between old and new paradigms

Key points at which the old and the new paradigm worlds collided and created challenges for the College were in finance and law. Suppliers of food and energy, for example, charged us the same as they charged everyone else. Similarly, staff expected salaries equivalent to those they could command elsewhere and for provision to be made for their pensions. At the same time there were volunteer staff offering their services as a gift, and we had students who could not afford to pay course fees and who received bursaries. On the other hand, in terms of employment law (and permanent staff were employees of The Dartington Hall Trust), there had to be precision about terms of employment such as the hours worked or holiday entitlement. Yet the College required and depended on a more flexible and generous attitude. As an example of this staff are provided with 'free' meals and in return are expected to spend the mealtimes with the students.

Within the College there are different kinds of jobs, some demanding slavish attention to the telephone and the outside world, others allowing freedom about when the job is done. After morning meeting each day, most staff led a morning work group before settling to their primary roles. This pattern of work raised significant questions. Was cleaning lavatories equivalent in value to handling reception? Was time spent doing this given voluntarily, or was it a part of the contracted work hours? Was simply being present at the College, eating a meal, truly work? Was a half-day on Sunday welcoming participants equivalent to an afternoon at the desk? Should you be able to trade one against the other? There could be a spirit of give and take within the College, yet still there remained the chance of misunderstandings between staff about the amount of 'work' that colleagues carried out and how they were rewarded. Further, when staff within the rest of the Trust and the College staff found themselves working together, the differences between the two cultures became apparent.

To some extent the College sat uncomfortably between the new and old paradigm worlds. On the one hand the Trust played by old paradigm standards in its employment of staff: there were benefits as well as disadvantages to this. On the other hand the new paradigm values of equality, service and compassion played themselves out in the learning environment of the College. Confusion emerged when the values of one realm slipped unnoticed into the other.

Reliance on high-profile scholars-in-residence

Throughout the College's history it has had well-known published writers as its scholars-in-residence. This was largely because it was they who made explicit in their works the ideas of the new paradigm and would attract students to attend the courses. Such people are often regarded with something approaching reverence, and some refer to them as gurus. There is sometimes criticism that the College is employing incongruent old-paradigm methods to study the new paradigm. Those who do not question that such inspiring individuals have much to teach us, dismiss this attitude as 'New Age hubris'. Others with a deep belief in 'learning' as opposed to what they describe as 'education', say that people learn by finding out things for themselves and there is no need for a teacher at all. In practice, the College offers a blend of the two diverse approaches. Pragmatically we accept that high-profile writers attract most students and that they have a significant place in shifting people's thinking. On the other hand we also contend that the College's processes are designed to promote deep learning.

In summary, the major challenge for those of us at the College was always to keep focused on its primary purpose of offering a programme exploring the foundations of the new paradigm, an ecological and spiritual worldview. As far as was possible we tried to ensure that the College's practices were congruent with that worldview.

Focal points

- Translating an idea into form and announcing our intentions to the world exposes us to criticism. The College is an expression of our understanding of the new ecological and spiritual paradigm. It inevitably reflects the limitations of our understandings, and the constraints on the design which come from having to operate within an old-paradigm world.
- Perhaps we have to be satisfied with being 'good enough' and use the paradoxes we face as opportunities to develop our own understandings.

Chapter 11

General conclusions

"The value of the College is extensive, but a word on two features that make it particularly important. First, Schumacher College operates at the frontier of ideas now becoming mainstream and moving the global society toward sustainability. The College has served as an incubator for many of the most creative minds of the past half-century."

– David Orr, frequent Scholar-in-Residence

This chapter summarises the conclusions we reached during the College's first years about what had been the formative influences from our particular environment on its establishment and evolution. It is not suggesting that all the circumstances need to be replicated when another centre is established. Rather, this list might provide food for thought as your plans develop.

The lessons learned at Schumacher College about setting up a centre for ecological and spiritual studies are transferable not only to other such centres, but also, in part at least, to other kinds of educational establishment.

- A key issue is that there needs to be congruence between WHAT is being 'taught' and HOW it is being 'taught' in order that students 'learn' what is intended. Thus, for example, whatever studies or activities are undertaken at Schumacher College, they must speak of the College's ecological and spiritual inspiration.

- It is arguable that many of the global problems the College set out to explore remain unresolved, as it is difficult to see that the international community is on course to avert ecological disaster. It seems likely that significant change will come from an unpredictable direction, rather than through a conventional state-led crisis management system. Effective change is likely to be an emergent phenomenon, such as a concerned civil society taking matters into its own hands. The kinds of people able to deal with the challenges posed in the twenty-first century are likely to have had experience and success learning in a context where emergence is promoted and encouraged.

- A community which creates opportunities for students to engage with other adults in sustained conversation about matters of vital interest, performs an important catalytic function which can be extended into students' own lives. In the way we live today, individuals are normally socially isolated, in nuclear family units, where the demands are such that we lack both the energy and the opportunity to engage with others in taking a part in developing creative and broad-based solutions to local and global ecological problems. At Schumacher College, life is designed to stimulate such conversation.

- In our case, the simple idea that was transformed into Schumacher College took root because the soil in which it was planted had been richly fed over the decades by a wide variety of intellectual, spiritual and practical sources. In this environment there was a willingness to invest in the exploration and development of new ideas. There were also enough resources to fund the investigations for, and the setting up of, the new College and for a period to cover its deficits while it put down strong roots and built a reputation for its work.

- The framework from which the College grew was built up gradually through a painstaking exploration of the new ecological and spiritual paradigm by a small core of individuals.

- A group containing several people who together had a range of the skills needed to design and bring about the practical expression of a theoretical idea, was supported by The Dartington Hall Trust to work intensively over an extended period to create the College.

- It was important to remember and to maintain a clear focus on the identity and purpose of the work. This entailed creating and sustaining a style of operation that spoke of the ethos and values of the College and manifested the spirit of the place. In its focus it offered intellectual challenge, spiritual exploration and emotional safety.

- Business skills such as marketing and fund-raising are essential ingredients of the skills mix required to build and run such a place. No matter how good the work is, students need to know about the place in order to find their way here.

- Given that numbers of individuals who might benefit substantially from attending courses cannot afford to do so, funds have to be raised to assist them.

- It is necessary to employ sheer hard work over extended periods and in the face of various setbacks while establishing and running such a venture.

- It is important to try to build an influential body of supporters for the work in order to enhance its credibility, to sustain it economically, and provide a sounding-board about proposed developments.

- The building allocated to the College was appropriate to a 'human-scale' activity. Each of the core activities of the College can have its special place in the communal space of the Old Postern. The kitchen and dining room are of the sizes needed to serve the needs of the number of people it takes to fill the bedrooms. One average person is able to lift a pan filled with the soup that will feed the typical resident population of the College. There is space in the Central Hall for morning meetings and evening celebrations, and the library with its fire is a perfect space to hold welcoming meetings at the start of courses. At first the meditation room was placed in a quiet space outside the main building but after the review it was brought into the heart of the College where it would remind everyone of the essential spirit of the College's work. Office functions were relegated to smaller rooms and less central spaces, again to highlight the real purpose of the College. The question of scale constantly exercises my mind. I do not want to think that only establishments not exceeding the magic number of about fifty-five or sixty members could work in this humane way. It would be interesting to apply the principles in a larger group, but my instinct is that once the provision of food cannot be handled by the community, then something critical is lost. I wonder whether there is an alternative activity (maybe meditation?) which would create a focal point for the group.

  Whatever the answer about the aspects that will hold a community together, there is a powerful case to be made that an activity and its accommodation should be in harmony.

- Satish Kumar's involvement has been vital to the College's work. Not only has his personal spirit informed the way the College has been designed, but in his regular presence he embodies and makes explicit the values of the place. Through his editorship of *Resurgence* magazine and his speaking tours around the world he has inspired many of the students coming to the College. There is some contention over whether a project such as Schumacher College needs someone such as Satish at its head. Wolfgang Sachs argues strongly that it does (see Chapter 14). On the other hand the world is not full of Satishes, and one would like to think that within a group setting up a project there might be manifested all the relevant qualities and attributes. Indeed there is something to be said for avoiding what can be seen as an old-paradigm patriarchal model, in which all the qualities to which the community aspires are expressed in a key charismatic leader. Wolfgang argues the contrary. He points out that the Jesuits, who for centuries have focused on preparing the next generation of minds, have always selected a charismatic leader to head their seminaries. He says that in contrast the Green Movement has failed to take responsibility to develop its next generation of leaders.

- In trying to grasp the spirit in the College, people have said to me that it is "very British". I did not take this as a criticism. Like a fish in water, I find it difficult to see the qualities of the water I live in. However, the ecological principle of 'thinking globally and acting locally' must apply when designing a new learning environment, rather than promoting slavish commitment to a model from elsewhere.

As a true product of a 1960s university education, I have always wondered whether the control exercised, be it as puppet master, '*deus ex machina*' or plain old-fashioned headmistress, to maintain the model designed all those years ago, is at odds with the spirit of the Thomas Berry quotation in the first chapter of this book (pp.21-2). Then I remind myself of the words of T. S. Eliot in *The Four Quartets*, 'Little Gidding':

What we call the beginning is often the end
And to make an end is to make a beginning.
The end is where we start from.

Chapter 12

The emergence of creativity at Schumacher College

A conversation between Fritjof Capra and Satish Kumar

One way to describe the processes at Schumacher College is as efforts to promote creativity. Fritjof Capra, one of the regular scholars-in-residence at the College met with Satish Kumar, the College's Director of Programmes, to probe the emergence of creativity through the environments designed at the College.

* * *

FC I am interested in the question: how can you design environments that foster creativity? It seems to me that Schumacher College is such an environment where people are very creative – not only the faculty, but also the course participants. I wonder whether you designed it with creativity in mind?

SK This is indeed an issue, but it is not so explicit. The creativity is there because the pedagogy of Schumacher College is based on education not from the outside in, but from the inside out.

FC What do you mean by that?

SK You don't see your students as empty vessels, to be filled with education, ideas and knowledge. The Schumacher teachers are generally interested in who the course participants are: what are their interests and qualities.

FC   And they emphasise dialogue. That's a very important feature of the courses.

SK   Yes, and dialogue sparks creativity. It's like when you plant a tree, you can give food, water and shelter to the seed, but the tree is in the seed. It has to come out of the seed, and that's the creativity.

FC   Yes. Another point is that on a Schumacher course it's not a dialogue between two people – one student and one teacher.

SK   Right. It's a collective dialogue, and you are trying to pool your collective ideas, rather than pushing individual ideas, as in a debate. It's a dialogue in terms of exploration. This is where the creativity is sparked.

FC   Now, when you have a dialogue, this means that you collectively look at things from various perspectives. You don't debate; you examine and explore things from different perspectives. And because of the tremendous diversity of the course participants, we always look at things from many different perspectives. With people from literally all parts of the world, you always have all these different viewpoints. That also stimulates creativity.

SK   Absolutely.

FC   Satish, when you meet with groups of students at Schumacher College, you first meet them in the kitchen, while cooking a meal. Why did you choose the kitchen for that first round of teaching? Is there a dialogue in the kitchen?

SK   Yes, there is a dialogue, but it is not just verbal. It is a dialogue with the materials. The way I am organising and co-ordinating the work to be done – how the sauce is made and how the rice is cooked – I emphasise a kind of empathy with the food. So I am teaching them how to relate to the materials, rather than just cooking to feed the people.

FC   In a sense you are expanding the community and including the food in the community, which indeed comes from another living community, from an ecosystem.

SK   Exactly. So the food serves not only to feed the body. It also creates a bonding and a belonging. The group comes together, and they feel that we are working together. Everybody supports the communal effort of creating this meal, which comes together from this collective effort. No individual has made it. I did not cook the dinner, because somebody else chopped the vegetables, somebody brought the oil, somebody brought that.

FC   That's what I would call the nature of emergence. Something emerges out of complex network activities.

SK   Exactly. This is in a way what I am teaching – the emergence out of complexity. But that complexity also has simplicity. For me, complexity and simplicity are not in contradiction: they are complementary. Through simply being together, supporting individuality and reciprocity, we are creating something.

FC   You are creating a meal; so there's the creativity.

SK   Yes, and the emergence. We don't know exactly what is going to emerge.

FC   Right. Now when you start, you don't know the participants. How do you start the teaching?

SK   We gather around the food in the middle, on the table. And I say, this is food. It is going to nourish our whole community; and there is a process of alchemy here. This raw potato, raw onion, raw garlic, raw grains of lentil and rice – you cannot eat them as they are; but we are going to transform them with fire, with our hands and with our imagination. Co-operatively working together we are going to transform these separate entities and bring them together in a balance – transform them into something which is beyond each individual item.

FC   So you tell them that. And then the participants focus their attention on it; they experience it and become aware of it.

SK   Yes, and then I talk about the fact that what is important when we are cooking is not just the process of cooking, but also the quality of attention. Just like meditation is not just sitting down with closed eyes, but paying attention, being mindful, being aware of what you are doing. Similarly, what is important in the kitchen is your whole presence there. And so the kitchen becomes the classroom.

FC   I also think, Satish, that this addresses different kinds of intelligences. People who are brilliant on the course are not necessarily those who are brilliant in the kitchen.

SK   Absolutely. Also when you are cooking, you are not only cooking with attention and meditative mindfulness; you are also cooking with heart. I would call this the 'alchemy of love'. You are expressing your love through the food. You are going to feed the community, and the feelings you have for the community go into the food. If your heart is not there, if you are feeling this is a duty and your mind is elsewhere, the food will not be nourishing.

FC   When you create something collectively – either the meal in the kitchen, or an idea in the classroom – that also needs trust in the community. Maybe that's another design element at Schumacher College. By nurturing community and by having people experience community in a very intense way, that creates a climate of trust and therefore a ground for creativity.

SK   Absolutely. Trust is the key. Most of our daily activities are based on choosing, analysing, planning and are often based on fear. But the moment you begin to trust, you lose your fear; and the moment you lose your fear, your creativity is no longer blocked. The blockage is removed. You can let go and trust that things will emerge. Then the creativity is coming through you, not from you. You become part of that process.

FC   Now, while they are cooking there are other conversations going on. Does that happen right from the beginning?

SK   Yes. I actually cook with participants on three Mondays. On the first Monday people get to know each other, where do you come from?

What have you studied? And so on. That is a more superficial introductory conversation. But in the second week the dialogue becomes deeper. You go deeper into ideas, into relationships.

FC   Of course, by that time, they are also well into the course and have had deeper dialogues in the classroom.

SK   Yes, and that small community of five people cooking also meets the next morning with me to reflect on the cooking, on the course, and on how this group is working together. So in this way, their cooking and their learning become connected.

* * *

The cooking activity is just one example of how staff take advantage of each opportunity to facilitate the learning of all the students. As each student at the College acquires the reverence and understanding to live in such a way as to have a positive environmental footprint, they are being empowered to make changes not only in one area of their lives but also to have the same potential in other aspects of their lives when they return home.

Chapter 13

Only Connect:
reflections on Schumacher College
by Vandana Shiva[29]

I came to England to give a Schumacher Lecture, and I really thought the work of the ecological movement needed a place where people could go beyond their narrow disciplines, their backgrounds, and learn about sustainability in a real life context. I wanted to do my bit to make it happen: that's why, when I learned about the establishment of Schumacher College I agreed to come. The reason why visiting and teaching at the College has become like an addiction for me is because the dialogues that take place here are, I think, at a very different pace from those in a typical conference setting. Questions are discussed here that no one can even raise in a typical academic setting. The College creates the space for a deeper reflection at a slower pace. I think that slow thinking always sounds like you're somehow retarded, but in reality fast thinking is no thinking at all. I always leave here with a clearer idea about the questions people have, and this allows me to communicate in different and more effective ways.

At a course in Schumacher College you have people from different countries and different backgrounds, with common interests but not a common jargon. Such students force me as the teacher to step back and look at the big picture (because that's what they are seeking), and at a communication level that is clear, that is not loaded and layered. The questions in the groups take you back to a street-level discussion, while they also force you to think in another way. Because of the diversity of their backgrounds, students are always seeking a combination of the intellectual and the activist. The participants here want those two connected, because they're all seeking to do things practically in their lives.

Now if you are in a G8 protest, everyone has their slogans; if you are in an academic system working on the political economy of globalisation, they've worked out the structure of the state and how it's been distorted by commercial interests; but when you are with a group that has combinations of people wanting to work on sustainability, the mixture then creates very interesting questions, because they want to know more about something that impacts their specialised field but is not part of the training that they have had. It just forces the teachers to put much more of their thinking in a coherent perspective.

I think there are two reasons why this interesting chemistry of creative questioning comes about at Schumacher College. The first is that there is a diverse mix of people with diverse backgrounds, but the second is that there has been a selection process in terms of who will apply. It's both the commonality and the diversity hanging together in a nice way. What you could have in a very mixed group is constant argumentation. That doesn't happen here, because everyone is seeking sustainability in a sincere way. I think another quality is that it's taking place in the context of the College, and this is what makes me give my time to it. I teach here for five days because of that shared and peaceful seeking of solutions.

I currently have a PhD student who was a student here at Schumacher College. She's now doing a PhD in Canada but comes to us (to Bija Vidyapeeth, the College I set up in India) for a substantial part of it. I meet people in different places who have been at my various courses. But what I love about this place is meeting people who came here as separate participants and later got married. This happens so frequently! Many of the course participants that have attended my courses have ended up eventually marrying someone they met here.

We modelled Bija Vidyapeeth very much on Schumacher College. The aspect in particular which is very different from other teaching institutions is that courses are based around a faculty, around particular themes, and are short-term, so that people can take a short time off their work to attend, if this is an interest that they want to pursue. We could have just done specialised long-term courses in the usual way, but instead we adopted the Schumacher model in covering a lot of ground on critical issues of our times. These are issues that don't get addressed much, but are concerning people. There's no place to turn to ask the questions, to find the answers and reflect deeper. That is why we need places like Schumacher College and Bija Vidyapeeth.

The second aspect we have adopted is the mixing of community work with learning. We call it Shram Daan, which means the gift of labour. The gift of labour includes the cleaning and the cooking – within a very different context, of course – but the inspiration is very much from Schumacher

College. Because we are in India, in addition we are able to add yoga classes, and because we're on the farm we are able to add practical farm work.

I think Schumacher College is such an important idea for our times because problems are getting created faster than university systems can even take them up. Our universities are stuck in time a hundred years ago in a way. Some of them are trying to be up to date but they're trying with a shallow response to big money. You know, MBAs are bursting everywhere. Training – voice training to man the call centres. India has become the capital of call centres: even British Rail gets its queries answered there. The young people are trained with accents to pretend that they're speaking from England, or from Texas or California. The schools for that sort of training are over-subscribed. But the real issues that matter ... How do we live in a way that reduces our carbon footprint? Or, How do we think about a life which is not based on reductionist biology? These issues that are going to determine the future of our species are not addressed. How many places are there that address them? That Schumacher does, is my reason to continue to return here, and it's the same reason that I started Bija Vidyapeeth.

Schumacher College has facilitated some important connections for the world! On one occasion when I had come to teach, Brian Goodwin had just moved here. Tewolde Egziabher and Martin Khor, both of whom later taught here, came to visit me and the four of us went for a walk and a talk in the Dartington Hall Gardens. Martin is an economist, head of the Third World Network, Tewolde is an ecologist and at the time was Secretary to the Environment Ministry of Ethiopia; Brian is a biologist, and I am a physicist and activist.

At the time, I and Tewolde were very involved with the whole genetic engineering question at United Nations level. In the dialogue with Brian an idea emerged that what we needed was a conference to look beyond reductionism, at the genetic engineering (GM) question. From that idea came the meeting which was called Beyond Reductionist Biology. In setting up the conference we pulled together four or five streams of people – the holistic biology community that Brian brings, the NGO community that's linked with the Third World Network (through Martin Khor), some of the ecologists that I and Tewolde knew, as well as people from genetic engineering. Out of that meeting grew a whole new level of the movement on genetically modified organisms. There was a community of biologists who knew that reductionist biology was wrong, but they were working on their little specialised topics. This meeting put these brilliant biologists together with economists, physicists and the activist movement.

That meeting of the best of cutting-edge science and the best of cutting-edge activism is what gave the anti-GM movement the life it has. Otherwise the activists would have been drowned by bad science and pushed out, and the scientists would never have been able to contribute in the way they did. This convergence of activism and science with a common agenda of speaking the truth about living systems definitely was born here at Schumacher College! Out of this meeting new coalitions were built. Someone like Tewolde met top scientists who could then bring environmentalists to the UN negotiations and first and foremost make the Biosafety Protocol happen. So it had the movements, it had the science and it had the United Nations, and it accelerated the impact of each hugely. Each of these separately would have been marginal to the debate. Despite one of the biggest, most powerful industries pushing a technology with such aggression, today much of the world is still GMO-free because of these interesting crossings and connections that could take place here at Schumacher College.

June 2007

Chapter 14

Building a non-conformist elite: reflections on Schumacher College
by Wolfgang Sachs[30]

From the point of view of a teacher, it is very rewarding to be together with a group of a reasonable size, say up to twenty-five people, for five or six days as is common at Schumacher College. It is very unusual in the entire educational landscape, that one teacher is together with one group for five or six days. And I think that's an extreme advantage. For the teacher it's good – you get to know people – and for the students too.

You need to get to know them because among the students you have various backgrounds, geographical regions, professional backgrounds, and a wide spread in age. Once there was a girl about twenty years old – I believe she was doing agriculture in Cornwall – and at the same time we had a seventy-nine-year-old man; a spread of about sixty years among participants. Again, that's something extraordinary: you don't have that in any other setting. If the spread is large enough, that is excellent. And I like that: to be intimately together for a week, to have these varied geographical and professional backgrounds, and the spread in age.

Now, apart from that, there is the overall setting that people participate in, and the work they do together like the kitchen work and cooking, and everybody eating together which forms a community. Maybe I should say that when I was teaching in the university I always tried – even when I was holding a normal course – to have an instance, mostly one weekend during a semester, where I went out with the entire course to some place outside. The best thing was to have a hut or a small hostel – the very best thing was if you had to care for your own subsistence. If you had to cook and you had to do things, that mixture of organising yourself, organising your subsistence and then discussing intellectual work – that is an extremely fertile mixture, because people get access to each other on very different levels. In a way I rediscovered that here at Schumacher College.

Also, I like the idea of being a modest part in building a non-conformist elite in the world. I see that Schumacher College is a place for the formation of a dissident elite and I like to see myself participating in that work. And now, I have been here to teach many times and I always have the feeling that it is a good way to spend my time. I always go home feeling, 'That was worth it!'

The overall philosophy of the College is worldview-oriented. It is not in the first place an institute of planning and technology. I mean, it is akin to what I personally am about, having done theology, and lots of cultural history. But this approach has a downside. For some years now I have felt as if I'm trying to counteract this groundswell of opinion that says that technology is not enough. For instance, this morning we spoke about ecotechnology and by way of an introduction I said, "Here in this house I often hear people saying 'Technology is not enough.' But I tell you something – also worldview is not enough." I feel one has to counteract that tendency a little bit, though by and large, it is of course my kind of mindset as well.

Also throughout the years, you get to know people. Last week I was in Budapest – that is a connection that goes back to Schumacher College. The same happened in Chile, and has happened elsewhere. Here, you meet people, and people invite you to their communities, or in some other way there is a connection being established and maintained. That is very rewarding and productive. You could probably even extend that much more deliberately.

I was asked by two people I had met here, to speak for them in Budapest. They are very active in what is probably one of the most prominent NGOs in Hungary, called Protect the Future. This is an environmental and social NGO, not so much oriented towards mass campaigning, but towards research work, intellectual and educational work, and also some campaigning. If I am not totally mistaken, that group has maybe about twenty-five very active people and another thirty or forty around them. And now, for the second time they did what is called a Globe Fest. It was in one of the very central places, a large club, and was held partly in the open air, right in the centre of Budapest. They put on an exposition, several workshops and one or two larger plenary films. I participated in the larger plenary and in the workshops. In addition we had one meeting with the inner circle of that NGO. Very nice people, and again, I guess it's not wrong saying this – I even said it to one of them – I see them becoming an important stimulus or yeast for Hungarian society. I wouldn't be surprised in twenty years from now if that group of people occupied some little piece of the administration of the government of Hungary.

It's easy to say that others can set up something like Schumacher College. The difficulty is there's no Satish Kumar for others. And it will be an enormous crisis for Schumacher College when he is not there any more. There's no doubt about it. In a way that is the singular, most important, distinct feature of the place. All other institutions purposefully and deliberately de-personalise their operations. It is typical of any modern education to have places which are not dependent on any particular person. They're trying to refrain from that, whilst in a way, Satish is the 'ghost that hovers' over everything here, on many levels. And therefore his presence is the glue, a kind of glue which keeps this thing together and provides also the thread which runs through it.

There is reason to believe that the most stable and interesting institutions are those which are built not around a person but where a person is the mainstay of the institution. Maybe also one of the weaknesses of the present-day educational institutions is that they do not allow themselves any longer to be like that. In my view, they should be happy if they had somebody like Satish, because whatever your belief system is, it has to be embodied by somebody. It has to be incarnated; it has to be made visible; it has to be lived. The vision has to be reinterpreted – and this is particularly true for an old institution like the church. Now, education is pervaded by the notion that things have to be objective – all operations, and in the last instance, also all persons. So in a way, in as much as you look at education as a machine running on objective conditions, even persons are interchangeable. And that is exactly the opposite of how it should be.

I always regretted that all the attempts so far to make other Schumacher Colleges spring up seem to have failed. I believe there has been a weakness of the environmental movement in a very general sense to build institutions. And you know, the Jesuits knew it all along, for centuries! The point is that through this you get to shape the coming elite. What has the environmental movement done? They have done all kinds of things, they have occupied places, they have written papers, they have founded businesses. But founding educational institutions – not much of that. That's a pity! It shows that in a way they do not have the long vision of the Church. The Church thinks in centuries. So you know, an important contribution a given generation can make is to shape the next generation, and this is what Schumacher College is doing.

June 2007

Chapter 15

Some other observations

David Orr is best known for his pioneering work on environmental literacy in higher education and his work in ecological design. He has taught here several times, and is another teacher whose perspective on our work is particularly valued because of the nature of his expertise. This was his reply to my request for comments.

Dear Anne,

You asked for a few words about the value of Schumacher College and I am glad to say that the College is a remarkable place. I first visited in the 1990s and have been back four or five time since. Each time has been unique both for the quality of the programmes and the quality of the students. You have an extraordinary faculty drawn from all over the world. I've been honoured to work with a few, co-teaching courses and related events.

The value of the College is extensive, but a word on two features that make it particularly important. First, Schumacher College operates at the frontier of ideas now becoming mainstream and moving the global society toward sustainability. The College has served as an incubator for many of the most creative minds of the past half-century. I don't know how many books, articles, and other projects were spawned at the College, but the number would be astonishing. Second, the College has attracted some of the most extraordinary students I've had the privilege to know. The alumni list of those students increasingly reads like a Who's Who in numerous fields. I've run into former Schumacher students in some very important places.

I am a supporter of the College, believe in its mission, and wish it prosperity and long life. More importantly the world needs Schumacher College and similar institutions around the world.

Warm regards,

David W. Orr, Paul Sears Distinguished Professor of Environmental Studies
Oberlin College, July 29 2007

David Cadman, student, helper and teacher at the College has reflected on his long association with it:

> Like most good ideas, it is quite difficult to recall how it all came about. It is almost as if it was always like this. But I do remember that a lot of thought went into trying to get right the balance between life at The Old Postern, and the courses that would be attractive enough to fund the venture. The focus on Ecology with Everything was always there – Science and Ecology, Business and Ecology, Arts and Ecology, Ecology and Ecology! And, of course, there was the reference to the teaching of Fritz Schumacher and, of great importance, the wisdom that Satish brought from his own experience of living in a religious community, the spirit of the monastery and the ashram, if you like. I seem to recall that from the very beginning, we wanted to reach out into the worlds of work and, not least, business, and that we wanted a wide variety of people to be brought together – men and women, young and old, people from near and far.
>
> But if my memory of the beginnings is poor, my memory of what it meant to be at Schumacher is good. Over many years, I visited Schumacher regularly – as a course participant, as a helper, on retreat, and even once or twice as a teacher. Best of all was to be a helper, as this rooted me firmly into the daily routine of the College. There were, of course, wonderful scholars and substantial teaching but for me, and I think for many others, the really important part of what we might call the 'Schumacher Experience' was the rhythm and depth of the daily life – the morning meditation, breakfast, housework, preparing meals, lots of washing-up, and endless cups of tea and conversation. If you could put that in a bottle and sell it worldwide, Mother Earth would be in much better shape!
>
> Best of all was the morning meditation. It was not always easy to get up at 6.30 a.m. to be ready and 'in place' by 7.00 a.m., but it was always worthwhile and, above all else, I remember some especially deep moments of Silence. In a world devoted to pace and 'entertainment' it is, perhaps, extraordinary that this should be so. And yet it is. So my anecdote is Beloved Silence and the friendship of those who work together in Love.

Stephen Sterling: a student, helper, teacher, reviewer of the College, and now a link with the University of Plymouth, wrote:

> TV ads some years ago, liked to use a 'before' and 'after' device, to show the efficacy of say, a soap powder. A crude analogy perhaps, but there are many stories from past participants of the College, that their experience was such that they felt significantly moved or changed as a result of being on a course: that they felt some form of transformation between 'before' and 'after', and, not uncommonly, in a

direction they did not anticipate. My own experience differs from most partici-pants in that I've enjoyed (and that's the right word) a relationship since 1993, when I first went on a course – with Fritjof Capra. Since then, I have been a par-ticipant in a further course, facilitated three others, been a tutor on three more, and been a College helper. I also wrote much of my doctoral thesis at the College, using its rich library and interacting with participants and tutors over a number of years. Also, in 2002 and with a colleague, I conducted a review of the Schumacher learning experience, based on interviews and questionnaires, resulting in a 20,000-word report. I feel most fortunate to have had this relationship, which, rather than being life-changing through exposure to just one course, has – rather – been dia-logical and interactive over a period of years. I have felt at various times affirmed, challenged, deepened, extended – and always welcome. My relationship with the College led to me looking much more deeply at systemic and ecological thinking; provided intellectual grounding to my doctoral thesis regarding how this thinking relates to changing our educational culture towards sustainability; and gave me the courage to write the (2001) Schumacher Briefing on Sustainable Education. In essence, the relationship has been critical to my ability to develop a strong intellec-tual and philosophical platform for asserting an holistic and ecological view of the emerging field of 'education for sustainability' where I have put my professional energies for many years. Like many who cross the threshold of the College, I was already fairly sure of my pathway, but my experience of the College has lent a depth, clarity and supportive energy to my professional and personal work that, I suspect, could not have been found anywhere else. For the record, I now find myself as Schumacher Reader in Education for Sustainability, at the Centre for Sustainable Futures, at the University of Plymouth, happily responsible for linking the College and the University in a positive collaborative partnership.

The Deep Ecology platform

This is a modification of Arne Naess's original platform, and was developed at Schumacher College in a course in 1995 led by Arne Naess, working with Stephan Harding.

1. All life has value in itself, independent of its usefulness to humans.

2. Richness and diversity contribute to life's wellbeing and have value in themselves.

3. Humans have no right to reduce this richness and diversity except to satisfy vital needs in a responsible way.

4. The impact of humans in the world is excessive and getting worse.

5. Human lifestyles and population are key elements of this impact.

6. The diversity of life, including cultures, can flourish only with reduced human impact.

7. Basic ideological, political, economic and technological structures must therefore change.

8. Those who accept the foregoing points have an obligation to participate in implementing the necessary change and to do so peacefully and democratically.

Notes

1. *Thomas Berry* is a Catholic priest, a cultural historian and an eco-theologian. He is author of many books including *The Dream of the Earth* (1988) quoted here and, with Brian Swimme, *The Universe Story* (1992). He taught at the College in 1995.

2. *Leonard and Dorothy Elmhirst and the Dartington Hall School.*

Dorothy Elmhirst (Founder-Trustee of The Dartington Hall Trust) Dorothy Whitney Elmhirst was born Dorothy Payne Whitney in Washington, USA in 1887. Her father, William Collins Whitney, was a well-known financier, statesman and connoisseur of the arts, and her mother, Flora Payne, was from a wealthy family of high social standing. Her mother died when Dorothy was six, and her father died in 1904, leaving Dorothy at the age of seventeen an extraordinarily wealthy and independent woman. She became actively committed to social welfare, and was involved in organisations like the suffragettes and the Women's Trade Union League. In 1911 Dorothy married Willard Straight, moving with him to Peking until the overthrow of the Manchu dynasty forced their return to America. Willard died in 1918 from pneumonia, having enlisted to serve in the first world war, leaving Dorothy a widow at thirty-one with three children, Whitney, Beatrice and Michael. Dorothy continued to be involved in social, educational, industrial and economic enterprises. In 1920 she met Leonard Elmhirst, son of an English clergyman and a student at Cornell University. Over a period of years Leonard courted Dorothy, and together they planned their experiment in education, research, rural regeneration and the arts. They married in 1925 and purchased Dartington Hall in Devon, England to start their enterprise. Two further children were born, Ruth and William. Dorothy died in December 1968.

Leonard Elmhirst (Founder-Trustee of The Dartington Hall Trust)

Leonard Knight Elmhirst was the second of nine children born to a York-shire parson. He read history at Trinity College, Cambridge. In 1915, he accepted a position serving with the YMCA in Mesopotamia and India, and subsequently became the private secretary to a Presbyterian missionary administering an agricultural college in Allahabad. After the first world war, Leonard attended Cornell University in New York, studying new, scientific methods of farming. He received a degree in Agricultural Economics and in 1921 was appointed by the Bengali poet Rabindranath Tagore to direct an agricultural school in a small village that was besieged by monkeys and mosquitoes. Tagore, however, could not pay him, and his salary and many of the operating expenses of the school were paid by the progressive philanthropist, Dorothy Whitney Straight, whom Leonard had recently met.

Leonard married Dorothy in 1925, and they purchased the near-derelict estate of Dartington Hall the same year. Both Leonard and Dorothy became trustees at Dartington Hall when they established the Trust in 1931. Leonard died in 1974.

Dartington Hall School

Leonard and Dorothy had enormous faith both in the importance of education and in Bill Curry himself when he came to Dartington in 1931 to head up Dartington's educational activities. What he created at the school has come to represent to people what progressive education is about. In 1931, Curry introduced residential accommodation shared by both sexes: unusually, co-education had been at Dartington from the start. He introduced conventional subjects. Generally, his staff were politically left, pacifists, agnostics and free-thinkers, with a strong sense of individualism. There was no form of dogmatic religious instruction because it was seen to be an obstacle to the development of a 'rational temper'. They believed there was a need to remove exams and other social pressures, arbitrary authority and attendant punishment, in order that the school would produce adults who were less cruel, more constructive and less aggressive than the norm. Alongside his work to bring about a peaceful federalist Europe, Curry's passion was to develop people who had initiative, self-respect and who were less docile and more peaceful than those conventionally educated. Everyone connected with the school believed that freedom and good feeling were more important than good behaviour, that school government needed to be reduced to a minimum, that class distinctions were minimised and informality was encouraged.

3. *Rabindranath Tagore* (1861-1941) A great Bengali humanitarian, social reformer and philosopher. An accomplished artist, he was mainly known for his poetry and received the Nobel prize for literature. He became a spiritual inspiration to his people.

4. *James Hillman* Archetypal psychologist, psychotherapist and visionary. Author of *A Hundred Years of Psychotherapy and the World's Getting Worse*, Hillman has taught at the College several times, first in 1995.

5. *Maurice Ash* (1917-2003), Chairman of The Dartington Hall Trust 1972-1984. Chairman of Town and Country Planning Association, Chairman of the Green Alliance. He suggested the name of Schumacher for the new College.

6. *Victor Bonham Carter* (1913-2007) carried out a detailed review of The Dartington Hall Trust for the years 1925-56.

7. *Mark Braham* was based at Dartington in the 1970s as a Scholar-in-Residence. He was a philosopher of education. He set up and ran the New Themes in Education Conferences at Dartington and it was he who first brought Henryk Skolimowski (below) to Dartington.

8. *Henryk Skolimowski* was at Dartington from 1976 to 1986, and is an ecophilosopher. He was philosopher-in-residence from 1978 to 1983, and set up a series of conferences and lectures here.

9. Thanks to Thomas Berry. In a lengthy bibliography in *The Dream of the Earth*, all these seminal texts (and many others) are mentioned.

10. *Satish Kumar* became a Jain monk in India at the age of nine. Inspired by Bertrand Russell's stand against atomic weapons, he left India on a peace walk to the four atomic capitals of the world. He settled in London and later became Editor of *Resurgence* magazine. He set up the Small School in Hartland, and was a member of the group designing Schumacher College. He is the author of several books including *No Destination: an autobiography* and *Spiritual Compass: the three qualities of life*. He is Director of Programmes at Schumacher College.

11. *E. F. Schumacher* (1911-1977), economist and statistician. He proposed human-scale and appropriate technologies. Based on his essay 'Buddhist Economics', his book *Small is Beautiful* is claimed to be one of the hundred most influential books since the second world war.

12. *John Pontin* was Chairman of The Dartington Hall Trust for thirteen years, during which time the College was created. He has a keen interest in sustainability and ecology.

13. *John Lane*, a member of the group designing the College, was a Trustee at Dartington during the time of Maurice Ash's Conferences and the birth of the College. He is a painter and writer, as well as a teacher and administrator.

14. *Brian Nicholson* was the last Head of Dartington Hall School. His academic background was as a research chemist, but he was also very interested in the work of Krishnamurti and taught at his school, Brockwood Park.

15. *Anne Phillips* is the author of this book. She was project manager of the group that originally planned the College, and was College Director from 1993 until she stepped down in 2006. Prior to this she had taught at Dartington Hall School, and been involved in curriculum development and project management in The Dartington Hall Trust.

16. *Lord Young of Dartington* (Michael Young), 1915-2002. Social innovator and writer of the 1945 Labour Party Manifesto which won them the first election after the war. He founded the Consumer Association; launched the prototype of the Open University; founded the 'University of the Third Age', and the 'School for Social Entrepreneurs'. He was a Trustee of The Dartington Hall Trust from its inception until 1992.

17. *Brian Goodwin* studied Biology at McGill University, Maths at Oxford University, and received a PhD in Biology from Edinburgh University. His best-known book is *How the Leopard changed its Spots*, published in 1994. He came to teach at Schumacher College from being Professor of Biology at the Open University, and was the first Co-ordinator of the MSc in Holistic Science.

18. *Julia Ponsonby* came to the College as a student on the first course and eventually became responsible for the catering here. In 2000 her recipe book *Gaia's Kitchen* was published, which has since sold over 10,000 copies. In 2001 it won an award as the best vegetarian cookbook in any language.

19. *David Orr* chairs the Environmental Studies programme at Oberlin College in the USA, and is known for his pioneering work on ecoliteracy in higher education. He speaks widely about sustainability. Two of his books are *Ecoliteracy* and *Earth in Mind*. He considers that environmentalism is 'a matter of ethical design'. He has taught at the College many times.

20. *David Cadman* is a birthright Quaker interested in language and how it shapes our lives. Professionally he is an urban land economist, and through this explores how we can live more lightly on the land. He has been a student at the College, a helper and a teacher, as well as contributing to early thinking about its development.

21. *Stephan Harding* studied zoology at Durham University and received his D.Phil in field ecology from Oxford. He is the College Ecologist, and was one of the original core faculty at Schumacher College. He began to work with James Lovelock on Gaia Theory after Lovelock's first visit to the College in 1991. He has also worked with Arne Naess on Deep Ecology. He is the author of *Animate Earth: Science, Intuition and Gaia* (2006), and he now co-ordinates the MSc in Holistic Science.

22. *The Dartington International Summer School of Music* (DISS) has been running since 1947. It is held in July/August each year for four or five weeks, and occupies residential space across the whole Dartington Estate.

23. *Fritjof Capra* is a physicist and systems theorist. He has written about ecoliteracy and has set up the Centre for Ecoliteracy in Berkeley, California. He is one of the College's Scholars-in-Residence, teaching here every other year since 1992. His best-known book is probably *The Tao of Physics*, written in 1975.

24. *Stephen Sterling* has been a student, helper, facilitator and teacher at the College. With a colleague he carried out a review of the College's work in 2002 for the Bureau of Environmental Education and Training. He wrote

the Schumacher Society's Briefing on *Sustainable Education*. His interests are in the interface between systemic and ecological thinking, learning and sustainability.

25. *Paul Roberts* is an organisational consultant currently working in Mexico on Leadership and Sustainability. He has been a student and facilitator at the College, and helped develop the College's modified design after the 1993 review.

26. *William Thomas* arrived just after the College opened, making a short visit to his sister Karen, who was one of the original core faculty. He has never left, and presently is House Manager, taking care of all the College's technical equipment. He holds most of the meditation sessions, and has the skill and stamina to MC the regular College soirées.

27. *Margaret Colquhoun* is a Goethean scientist who researches medicinal plants and landscapes using a holistic observational technique. She is Director of the Pishwanton Trust, which works on environmental issues in Scotland, and an occasional teacher on the MSc programme.

28. *Professor Peter O'Neill*, an environmental scientist, was the person who steered the MSc in Holistic Science through the validation procedures at Plymouth University.

29. *Vandana Shiva* has taught at Schumacher College most years since 1992. She is a physicist, ecofeminist and environmental activist. She participated in the Chipko movement, (hugging trees to prevent their felling), and has campaigned on many issues including globalisation, intellectual property rights, genetic engineering, biodiversity and organic farming.

30. *Wolfgang Sachs* is based at the Wuppertal Institute in Germany. He studied sociology and theology, and was a follower of Ivan Illich. His work is on globalisation, new models of wealth and notions of development. Perhaps his best known work is *The Development Dictionary*. He co-ordinated the group that produced the Jo'burg Memo for the 2002 UN Johannesburg Summit on Sustainable Development. He has taught at the College most years since 1994.

Index

Also available from Green Books

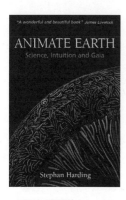

ANIMATE EARTH
Science, Intuition and Gaia

Stephan Harding

"This is a wonderful and beautiful book,
a teacher's treasure." – James Lovelock

"*Animate Earth* represents systems science at its best . . .
gives a whole new dimension to what 'environment-friendly'
really means." – Jonathon Porritt

In *Animate Earth* Stephan Harding explores how Gaian science can help us to develop a sense of connectedness with the 'more-than-human' world. His work is based on a careful integration of rational scientific analysis with our intuition, sensing and feeling—a vitally important task at this time of severe ecological and climate crisis.

Stephan Harding replaces the cold, objectifying language of science with a way of speaking of our planet as a sentient, living being rather than as a dead, inert mechanism. For example, chemical reactions are described using metaphors from human life, such as marriage, attraction, repulsion etc, so as to bring personality back into the world of rocks, atmosphere, water and living things. In this sense, the book is a contemporary attempt to rediscover *anima mundi* (the soul of the world) through Gaian science, whilst assuming no prior knowledge of science.

The Author: Dr Stephan Harding holds a doctorate in ecology from the University of Oxford. He is the Co-ordinator of the MSc in Holistic Science at Schumacher College, where he is also Resident Ecologist and a teacher on the short course programme.

Green Books ISBN 978 1 903998 75 5
224pp with illustrations, charts and diagrams £10.95 pb

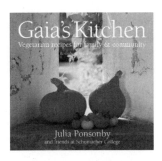

GAIA'S KITCHEN

Vegetarian Recipes for Family
and Community

Julia Ponsonby
and friends at Schumacher College

"I've eaten this food many times and have sat at the inviting table of its authors. I can say honestly that this book should have an honoured place in your kitchen and that your kitchen should be the most honoured room in your house. Follow its unconventional wisdom about food, and you will discover the secret to a rich and meaningful life."
– Thomas Moore, author of *Care of the Soul* and *Original Self*

"Food at Schumacher College is a world away from plastic food in a conference tray, or the fast food that most university students live on. It is 'family cooking' that, sadly, few families now manage. And it's healthy, hearty, and delicious. The recipes come in two sizes – for home cooks, and for caterers. I would recommend this book for anyone working in a school, a B&B, a pub, or running a community event – and of course for home cooks."
– Prue Leith, caterer, restaurateur and food writer

The cuisine featured in *Gaia's Kitchen* calls upon the best of Mediterranean, Californian, Indian, and Mexican vegetarian cooking. It celebrates old favourites rich in cheese and eggs, and offers a variety of tempting vegan dishes using ingredients such as pulses, tofu, and tempeh. Besides soups, main courses and salads, there's a mouthwatering selection of desserts, breads, cakes, and biscuits. *Gaia's Kitchen* also explores the issues of nutrition, special diets, and the ecological dimension of food production. The recipes are the tried and tested creations of Julia Ponsonby and her colleagues at Schumacher College in Devon, England, which since 1991 has been brewing up a unique *pot pourri* of human connections, raising ecological awareness, and stimulating taste buds. ***Revised and updated edition 2008.***

Green Books ISBN 978 1 900322 25 6
216pp with colour and b&w photos £14.95 pb

Gourmand World Cookbook Award Winner

Schumacher College

Transformative Learning for Sustainable Living

Schumacher College at Dartington has helped thousands of organisations and individuals in understanding and finding solutions for the most pressing ecological and social concerns of modern life. We are renowned for the excellent teachers that lead our courses.

The College seeks to offer a positive educational space which integrates the concerns of governments, NGOs, industry and individuals. Through a range of educational activities, participants are encouraged to consider some of the most urgent challenges of sustainability and to take responsibility for delivering effective solutions in their own working and personal environments. What and how they learn stays with them for a lifetime.

Inspirational course topics include:

Holistic economics
Strategies for creative social change
Sustainability and leadership
Earth jurisprudence
Systems thinking in practice
Championing sustainable food

For more information about our courses and other activities please visit our website

Dartington

Schumacher College is an initiative
of The Dartington Hall Trust
a registered charity